Read, Write, Play

HOW TO CREATE
LITTLE
HAPPY
LEARNERS
60 SIMPLE LEARNING and CRAFT ACTIVITIES for 0–5 year olds

Read, Write, Play

100 Easy Ways to Make Phonics Fun for Children Aged 2–7

Sophie David

ROBINSON

Also by Sophie David

How to Create Little Happy Learners

ROBINSON

First published in Great Britain in 2025 by Robinson

10 9 8 7 6 5 4 3 2 1

A CIP catalogue record for this book
is available from the British Library.

ISBN: 978-1-47214-990-9

Photography by Cristian Barnett
Illustrations by Sarah Weston
Designed and typeset in Silka by thextension

Printed and bound in Italy by L.E.G.O. S.p.A.

Papers used by Robinson are from well-managed forests
and other responsible sources.

Robinson
An imprint of
Little, Brown Book Group
Carmelite House
50 Victoria Embankment
London EC4Y 0DZ

The authorised representative
in the EEA is
Hachette Ireland
8 Castlecourt Centre
Dublin 15, D15 XTP3, Ireland
(email: info@hbgi.ie)

An Hachette UK Company

www.hachette.co.uk

www.littlebrown.co.uk

To Adam, my best friend and to Ted, Finn and Edie, my greatest achievements.

You are everything, and this book is for you.

Contents

Author's Note

I am absolutely delighted to share this book with you. It has been a dream of mine to create excitement and enthusiasm around learning through play, and phonics has been a huge passion of mine for as long as I can remember, so this, to me, is a match made in heaven. Before launching Little Happy Learners, I spent a decade working in education. I was a primary school teacher, early years specialist and phonics fanatic. I have dedicated my career to creating playful learning experiences and building a love of learning for all.

The inspiration for this book came from my love of phonics and my desire to make it more fun, enjoyable and accessible. Having experienced what it is like to have two of my own children take their first steps in mainstream education, I felt compelled to explore how parents and carers are introduced to the concept of phonics and felt deeply that there is not enough information readily available. I knew I needed to share my expertise with a wider audience. This journey has been both personal and professional, blending my passion for learning through play with my expertise in early education.

In 2019, I launched Little Happy Learners. Initially, it was a passion project to keep me busy while on maternity leave, but it very quickly became more. Today, Little Happy Learners is an online hub for parents, carers and educators around the world in which activities, ideas and educational tips are shared. I provide free learning resources and sell my own range of phonics flashcards. I am continuing to spread the message that learning should, above all else, be fun.

Throughout my career, I have been honoured to work with thousands of children, parents and educators, all of whom have fuelled my drive to make learning more playful! In 2024 I connected with more than 56 million people, all wanting to know more about phonics. How incredible!

When I am not writing or working on new, fun learning activities, I enjoy spending time with my three beautiful children; they are my inspiration and will always keep me grounded.

The tools and ideas in this book will help you to help your children learn to read, write and play I hope it provides you with all the information you need to get started on your own phonics playtime. For more insights and updates, you can connect with me on Instagram, @littlehappylearners, or visit my website at www.littlehappylearners.co.uk.

Thank you for embarking on this journey with me.

Sophie David, Little Happy Learners

Get Ready to Read, Write and Play

Read, Write, Play introduces the concept of the six phases of phonics. It begins with pre-reading skills for preschool-aged children and ends with the exploration of irregular plurals and suffixes. It is perfect for children aged two to seven. The six chapters share the crucial details of each phase and offer a range of activities designed to support the children in your care in a fun, simple and hands-on way.

The world of phonics can be overwhelming and daunting for any new parent, carer or educator. There is a lot of information out there, it's hard to find the answer to specific questions and it's even harder to find hands-on and engaging ways to play with phonics. Treat this as your go-to phonics guide.

Children learn best by doing, so in this book there are one hundred physical activities to enjoy with your children. Using simple household items, you can do every activity in five minutes or less. They are designed to fit around busy lifestyles and to be repeated time and time again.

Simple and creative strategies are presented as fun and engaging activities, which will enable you to overcome the tricky challenges children are faced with when reading and writing and help you to enjoy the process together.

Play and accessibility are at the heart of this book! I want everyone to be able to support their children on their phonics journey. It is so important to make learning fun. Enjoyable learning experiences boost children's intrinsic motivation: when children take pleasure in their learning, they are more likely to participate and invest their efforts.

Fun learning activities often involve multiple senses and active participation, which can in turn improve memory retention. Children are more likely to remember information if it is presented in a memorable way.

Here are my four key principles to play

There are four key principles to follow when introducing play-based learning that will make sure your play is effective and bring you and your child the most happiness and success.

1 Plan

Planning an activity into your day is where this all begins. Write a list of small, achievable activities that you can add into your week and tick them off as you go. So many of the activities in this book require little to no preparation and can be embedded into your daily routine.

2 Time

Find a ten-minute window of time with your little one(s) and ensure that you have nothing else to do. The washing can wait, put down all devices and play together. Children love to see us playing too, so get involved and enjoy.

3 Prepare

Prepare physically or mentally for each activity. Whether it is gathering resources or just taking a deep breath, make sure you are in the right frame of mind so that it's fun for all.

4 Reward

Who does not love to see their child learning something new? This is the reward for you. The reward for them: time spent with you, a fun activity and some new knowledge. What more could they ask for?

How to use the book

This book is broken up into the six phases of phonics. The phases have been colour-coded so you can find your way easily. Each chapter begins with a full explanation of the phase, ensuring that you have all the necessary information at your fingertips.

At the start of each chapter you will find a contents page, so you can effortlessly choose an activity that best suits your child's needs at any given time.

If in doubt, turn to page 18, where you will find a list of phonics terminology with a description. This should help with any confusion along the way.

There are one hundred activities throughout the book. Each activity covers an important aspect of phonics and uses a household item to make it hands-on and fun. Adapt the activities to suit what you have in and around your home, be creative and be resourceful. This book is designed to fit in and around your lifestyle.

Each of the activities are broken up under these headings:

Description – This is a quick explanation of what the activity entails.
What you need – Here you will learn everything that's required to complete the activity. I often give ways in which the activity can be changed, adapted and simplified.
Preparation – This will give you an idea about how long each activity will take to set up, and tell you what you need to do to get ready.
Activity details – This is how you will complete the activity with your child, what it will look like and what kinds of questions you could ask.
Idea bank – Lots of the activities have a word or idea bank. I've done the thinking, so you don't have to.

Keep your eyes peeled for some top tips along the way. Those snippets may just help your activity become a huge success!

This book can provide you with the tools to observe your child learn and grow. By revisiting the activities time and again, you will see how much your child has developed.

One of the many reasons I loved teaching Early Years was because of the huge amount of progress I witnessed in the children throughout the year. Our lives are so fast paced these days that we often forget to take in those moments of growth. I recommend getting a folder and placing all the activities you complete from this book in it. Then you can go back and see what you have both learned. It'll be a keepsake worth keeping.

What Is Phonics?

Phonics is a method for teaching reading and writing. It demonstrates the relationship between the sounds of the spoken language and the letters or groups of letters or syllables of the written language.

The National Literacy Strategy brought phonics to the forefront of teaching reading and writing in 1998. Before this, 'whole-word' and 'whole-language' approaches dominated teaching practices.

Using phonics, we can teach people how to read and write by showing them the sounds that letters and groups of letters make. Here is a simple breakdown:

- **Letters and sounds:** Each letter in the alphabet represents a specific sound. For example, the letter 'b' makes a **buh** sound.
- **Decoding:** Involves breaking down the sounds in words and blending them together for reading.
- **Blending:** You learn to put these sounds together to make words. For instance, the sounds **c**, **a** and **t** come together to make the word 'cat'. This is used for reading.
- **Segmenting:** You also learn to break words down into their individual sounds. For example, 'dog' can be broken down into **d**, **o** and **g**. This is used for spelling.
- **Fluency:** When children are secure in their learning, and when speed and accuracy increases.
- **Phases:** Phonics is broken up into **six phases**, with each phase concentrating on different skills. Children should be comfortable with what they have learned in one phase before moving on to the next. This helps to build fluency in reading and writing.

Phonics can be especially helpful for children who struggle with reading, as it provides clear rules and strategies for decoding words. However, not all children learn in the same way. Some might find phonics less engaging or may benefit more from other approaches that include whole-language learning, where they are exposed to reading through context, pictures and storytelling.

The practical, engaging activities in this book aim to support ALL children; they provide context and visual support and many of them follow a multi-sensory approach. Phonics can be for everyone!

The activities will work alongside your child's nursery, school or home education. The book follows the same structure and pace as most other phonics schemes and will fit hand in hand with school-based lessons.

Think of this as the perfect supplement to your child's education. You are providing them with the tools to play and enjoy phonics with you and independently.

The Six Phases

The six phonics phases are part of a structured programme often used in the UK to teach children how to read and write.

Phase 1
Sound awareness

(age two to four) – see page 22

Ability to hear and identify different sounds.

- Instrumental and environmental sounds.
- Rhyming.
- Alliteration.
- Beginning to segment and blend sounds orally.

Phase 2
Introducing simple sounds and letters

(age four to five) – see page 60

Recognising and writing the letters and sounds for **s, a, t, p, i, n, m, d, g, o, c, k, ck, e, u, r, h, b, f, ff, l, ll, ss.**

- Teaching one sound/letter per session.
- Blending sounds to form simple words (for example sat, pin, tap).
- Segmenting words into individual sounds.
- Using phonics games and activities like flashcards, magnetic letters and writing in sand.

Phase 3
More complex sounds and letters

(age four to five) – see page 104

Learning twenty-six new graphemes – **j, v, w, x, y, z, zz, qu** – and common digraphs and trigraphs – **ch, sh, th, ng, ai, ee, igh, oa, oo, ar, or, ur, ow, oi, ear, air, ure, er.**

- Practising blending and segmenting.
- Recognising, reading and writing more complex words.
- Developing fluency with blending sounds to read words.
- Practising reading and writing captions and sentences.

Phase 4

Consolidation (age five to six) – see page 148

Practising reading and writing words with adjacent consonants – **st, nd, mp, tr.**

- No new sounds introduced.
- Improved ability to read and spell words with multiple sounds.
- Learning more complex consonant clusters.
- Emphasis on reading and writing longer words and sentences.

Phase 5

Alternative Sounds and Spellings

(age five to six) – see page 188

Learning new graphemes for known sounds – **ay, ou, ie, ea, oy, ir, ue, aw, wh, ph, ew, oe, au.**

- Learning alternative spellings for words.
- Learning alternative pronunciations for graphemes – **a** (hat/acorn), **e** (bed/he), **i** (sit/find), **o** (hot/go), **u** (but/put), **ow** (cow/snow), **ie** (pie/chief), **ea** (seat/bread).
- Practising reading and spelling with these new patterns.
- Reading more complex texts and writing independently.

Phase 6

Fluency and Accuracy

(age six to seven) – see page 228

Focusing on spelling rules and patterns and the use of common word endings.

- Practising reading with increased speed, fluency and comprehension.
- Learning spelling rules and patterns; adding suffixes like **-ing, -ed, -er, -est, -y.**
- Focusing on common spelling rules and word endings.
- Encouraging independent reading and writing.

This is a very brief introduction to what is covered in each of the phases. Each chapter of the book covers one phase and each of the activities cover one element of the phase requirements. **Everything you need to know is contained within this book!**

Key Phonics Terms

Using terminology correctly with your child will help them to excel in reading and writing and develop a secure understanding of phonics. Many of the key phonics terms may be unfamiliar to you but the brief descriptions below will help you to introduce them to your child effectively. Children love learning new vocabulary!

Basic Phonics Terms

Blending – putting sounds together to say a word (used for reading).
Segmenting – splitting up and saying each individual sound in a word – also known as sound-talk, for example **c-a-t** (used for spelling).
Phoneme – the smallest unit of sound.
Grapheme – the written form of a sound, for example a letter.
Grapheme phoneme correspondence – matching the sound to the letter that represents it.

Types of Sounds

Initial sound – the first sound in a word.
Vowel – a speech sound produced without blocking the breath channel; vowels in English are a, e, i, o, u and sometimes y.
Consonant – all letters of the alphabet that are not vowels
Adjacent consonants/Consonant blend – a word with two adjacent consonants, for example hand.
Digraph – two letters that make one sound, for example **sh**ip and b**ea**ch.
Trigraph – three letters that make one sound, for example l**igh**t.
Split digraph – two letters split by another letter, where the two letters together make one sound: **a-e** in 'make' and **i-e** in 'bike' (sometimes known as 'magic e').
Alternative graphemes – different ways to write the same sound, for example **ai**, **a-e**, **ay**, **ei**, **eigh** and **ey** all make the **ai** sound.

Word Parts

Syllable – a unit of pronunciation with one vowel sound. Each syllable has at least one vowel. Cat has one syllable; rabbit has two syllables.

Onset – the initial consonant sound of a syllable, for example **c**at.

Rime – the part of a syllable that contains the vowel and all that follows it, for example c**at**.

Prefix – a group of letters added to the beginning of a word to change its meaning, for example **un**happy.

Suffix – a group of letters added to the end of a word to change its meaning or grammatical function, for example look**ing**.

Word Types

Noun – a word to identify objects, people and places, for example door, Adam, Australia.

Adjective – a word that describes a noun, for example brown.

Verb – an action word/doing word, for example dance.

Adverb – a word that describes a verb, for example noisily.

Monosyllabic words – words that contain only one syllable, for example dog, fish, purse

Polysyllabic words – words that have more than one syllable, for example armchair, dinosaur, butterfly.

Alliteration – words that have the same initial sound.

Rhyme – words that have the same end sound.

CVC word – a three-letter word that is made up of a consonant, then a vowel and then a consonant, for example cat.

Sight Words – words that cannot be sounded out and are used frequently. These words do not often follow the rules. It is a great idea to try to find a new rule or rhyme to remember together.

Supply List

Anyone can complete each of the activities in this book without buying a thing. You can use what you have in and around your home to set up wonderful engaging learning opportunities. You just need to know how.

All of the activities are accessible, require little to no preparation and use one of the ten items listed below.

Here are the top items that feature in all one hundred activities. It is not essential that you have exactly these items to hand; feel free to find simple swaps or alternatives from within your home.

Item	Alternatives
Paper cups	Any cups
White board and dry erase marker	Paper and pencil
Sensory tray or basket	Baking tray, bowls or pots
Playdough	Homemade playdough (see recipe on page 272)
Pompoms	Cotton wool balls
Building blocks	Duplo, Lego, wooden blocks, magnetic tiles or Mega Bloks
Craft sticks	Lollipop sticks, pegs, wooden stirrers or cotton buds
Cardboard tubes	Toilet rolls, kitchen rolls, rolled-up paper, rolled-up cardboard, guttering, pipes
Post-it notes	Paper squares
Magnetic letters	Cut-out letters, letter tokens, wooden discs, Scrabble tiles

These top ten items are extremely versatile. In my home, we have each of these resources in a 'phonics box' that we can grab at any time. This means that you too could have a hundred activities stashed away in a box, ready and waiting for you!

Some activities require picture prompts. If you do not own a printer, have a go at drawing some simple illustrations yourself. You do not need to be an artist to engage your children. Everyone is an artist in the eyes of their children.

AGE
2–4

PHASE 1

This chapter shares some wonderful ways that you can explore Phase 1 of the phonics journey. Phase 1 is often the forgotten phase, a whole chunk of learning that is left out entirely. However, it is of the utmost importance. This initial stage of your phonics journey holds the key to a successful and confident approach to reading and writing.

Before children learn to read and write, they need to develop their phonological and phonemic awareness: the ability to listen and identify sounds and understand how they come together to form words.

Phase 1 phonics facilitates and provides the gateway to early reading and writing. It is usually covered around the ages of two to four and it helps to prepare children to understand and use the alphabetic code, develop an understanding of sounds and provide a designated time for 'learning'.

Scan QR code for an optional resource shortcut!

Phase 1 looks at seven main aspects

Each of these seven aspects target specific abilities that collectively prepare children for their learning journey.

Environmental Sounds

This aspect looks at the sounds that we hear in our environment and develops children's listening skills by helping them to distinguish between different sounds.

Instrumental Sounds

Here we look at the sounds made by instruments and aim to develop children's ability to match sounds to their sources while exploring pitch and pace.

Body Percussion

This further develops children's awareness of sounds, looking at the way we can create different noises with our bodies. This looks to build understanding about rhythm and the ability to mimic and produce different sounds.

Rhythm & Rhyme

Familiarises children with rhythmic structures of spoken language, which supports their ability to recognise patterns and predict words which are both fundamental for developing phonemic awareness.

Alliteration

This aspect focuses on the initial sounds in words, which is a key skill in learning phonics and spelling. It helps with sound identification, which is the start of sounding and blending.

Voice Sounds

This encourages children to experiment with their voices, how they can make different sounds and how sounds are produced. It is important to look at our mouth movements and positions to enable us to learn sound discrimination accurately. See page 278 for accurate mouth positions and descriptions for each sound of the alphabet.

Oral Blending and Segmenting

This aspect is crucial in learning how to blend sounds together to form words. It is completed verbally and is essential in the reading process.

Before you can begin to teach your child to recognise letters and the sounds that they make, they need to develop listening and attention skills, vocabulary and language skills, and social and communication skills. All of which are at the core of the next sixteen activities.

Important information

- Children aged two have an average attention span of four to six minutes.
- Children aged three around six to eight minutes.
- Children aged four around eight to twelve minutes.

It is important to remember this when engaging in an activity with your child. Look to enjoy the activities multiple times, using short windows of time. You will get so much more from the experience.

LITTLE

Contents

Important information
Please remember that Phase 1 is mostly about *spoken* sound – looking at how we produce sounds with our mouths and what they sound like. It is not about the written form!

If you do want to look at letters please ensure they are all in lower case.

TOP TIPS

Always sit facing your child. This will help you when modelling and your child when mimicking.

Always ensure that the room you are playing in has no background noise (no TV or music).

Try to add their favourite toys into your games where possible, this will engage them for longer.

Begin with short activities and build up to spending longer windows of time together.

This chapter has been designed to be enjoyed by toddlers and preschool-aged children. There is no specific time frame or timetable for your child to complete Phase 1 phonics, so you can go at your own pace. Try to embed these short activities into your week and enjoy the little moments of connection.

Nature Sounds

This activity looks at Environmental Sounds. It involves making sounds with nature – rustling leaves, scraping sticks, picking petals, banging stones. Everything and anything can make a sound, but can you be quiet enough to hear it?

What you need

A basket, bowl or tray

Preparation

Make a checklist of natural objects. Go on a nature hunt with your child and see which objects you can find. Fill up your tray and head inside to a quiet area.

Activity 1

Explore the natural objects together. Label all of the objects and then direct your child to make different sounds. For example, you could bang two stones together or crunch the leaves.

This is great for developing understanding of different vocabulary, but it's also brilliant for listening and attention. Can your child listen to your instruction?

Activity 2

Prompt your child to close their eyes. Use the natural objects to make some different sounds. Can your child guess which object made each sound?

Bang
Snap
Crunch

Sound Walk

This activity covers Environmental Sounds. There are lots of noises all around us and if you step outside your house, you can hear even more. What noises can you hear?

What you need

A checklist of objects you think you might hear on your walk

Preparation

Before you head outside, ask your child what they think they might be able to hear when you go out for your walk today. Give them some examples but, most importantly, enjoy listening to their wonderful ideas. You will be amazed at some of their thoughts. On a piece of paper either draw or write some of your ideas and make it into a small checklist – this will help to keep you on track.

Activity

Head outside with your checklist and try to hear some of the different noises on your list. Prompt your child to close their eyes and focus on different sounds. If your child is in a pushchair, make sure you are looking at them when you are talking about the sounds. This will further enable your child to focus on their listening skills.

You can complete this activity time and time again – try doing it in different places at the beach, in the woods or near a busy town. You will hear different things every time.

IDEA BANK

Birds, dogs, ambulance, motorbike, police car, car, aeroplane, lorry, talking, children, wind, rain, lawnmower, water from a stream, music from a car

Sound Baskets

This activity covers Alliteration. Sound baskets are a brilliant way to explore the initial sounds in words. Simply fill a basket with lots of objects all beginning with the same initial sound. Every day can become a sound hunt in your house.

What you need

A basket, bowl or tray

Objects from around the home

Sound cards or handwritten letter cards

A bag

Preparation

Grab a basket, a sound card and a selection of objects beginning with the same sound. For example: scissors, toy spider, satsuma, spoon, string, sock, etc.
Place the objects in a bag.

Activity

Look at the sound card in the basket and ask your child if they know what it is. Tell your child what sound it makes and explain that you have found lots of objects that begin with that sound.

Prompt your child to pull one object out the bag at a time and say the word. Place the objects into the basket and leave the basket somewhere your child can access it throughout the day/week. They may want to practise again on their own.

TOP TIP
When saying each object's name, try to really emphasise the initial sound, for example **ssss**poon.

Note
This activity can be completed twenty-six times! You can try it with each letter of the alphabet separately, or do two or three sounds at the same time.

s
t
p

Music Tubes

This activity covers Instrumental Sounds. Musical instruments all make different sounds and exploring their sounds can be fun, but an even better way of exploring instruments is by making your own!

What you need

Cardboard tubes (the inserts of kitchen towels are best because they are longer)

Dry rice, pasta, chickpeas, lentils or whatever you can find that makes a distinctive noise

Tape

Pens

Preparation

Grab everything you need and away you go.

Activity 1

Making the music tubes is just as much fun as playing with them. Squeeze one end of the cardboard tube together to seal it shut, and use some tape to secure it. Fill your tube with your music maker (rice, pasta, etc.) and then secure the other end. You can use the pens to decorate the outside.

It is best to make two or three different music tubes so you can hear the different sounds they make.

Activity 2

Enjoy using your new musical instruments. Can your child tell you what is inside their tube? What does it sound like? How do they know it is rice, for example, rather than pasta?

Put on some nursery rhymes and explore playing your new instruments with the beat.

You could even try tapping your own beat for your child to mimic.

> **Note**
> If you do not want to use food produce you can fill your music makers with beads, stones or shells.

Matching Cups

This activity covers Alliteration. Every word begins with a sound, but can you hear the sound at the beginning of the word? This is a game of memory; can you remember where the correct object is hiding?

What you need

Two or three cups

Pictures of objects beginning with the same sound

Preparation

Grab some cups

Draw or print pictures of six objects: four beginning with the same sound and two that do not. For example, turtle, tambourine, tap, tiger, shark and pot.

Cut the pictures up so that they fit under the cups.

Activity

Hide three of the pictures under three cups. Make sure that two begin with the same letter and one does not. Can your child find the two matching sounds?

This activity focuses on the initial sounds in words, so it is important to accentuate the initial sound when working with your child.

Repeat the game with the other set of objects.

IDEA BANK

Pot	Spoon	Cat
Pig	Spider	Can
Pirate	Sock	Cot
Pen	Snake	Crab
Moon	Rock	Hedgehog
Flower	Net	Mop

Pompom Soup

This activity covers Initial Sounds and Alliteration. Water play is a guaranteed winning activity with preschoolers! Allow children to explore sounds and have some fun with this multi-sensory activity.

What you need

A large tray

Water

Coloured pompoms

Spoons

Bowls or cups

Preparation

Fill a tray with water and add some pompoms.

Activity

Explore the water tray with your child and look at how you can make some simple splashing noises. Reach for a coloured pompom and name the colour of the pompom aloud. Can your child name the colours of the rainbow? If not, work on labelling each of the colours together. This is a great skill to learn, it shows children that everything has a name.

If your child can name all the colours, develop their initial sound sense. Begin to highlight the initial sound in all the colours, for example '**y-y-y-y**ellow'.

While they are playing, label the colours and the initial sounds. You will be surprised how much children can retain while they are enjoying themselves.

House Hunt

This activity covers Oral Blending. Houses are filled with objects that we can name and sound out. We can turn everyday items into a fun game. Are you ready to go on a house hunt?

What you need

Craft sticks

Pictures of household objects

Tape or glue

Preparation

Draw or print some pictures of household objects.

Stick them to craft sticks.

Place the sticks in a cup.

Activity

Grab a stick and try to find it in your house. It is as simple as that. When your child finds the object, they must bring it to you and tell you the initial sound of the word.

Once your child has found all the objects, lay them out in front of them.

Using simple objects that only have three sounds in them (also known as CVC words) can you sound the word out and ask your child to select the correct object. For example, 'Can you find the **c-u-p**?'

Playdough Letters

This activity covers Letter Formation and Fine Motor Skills. Letters can be written or made with lots of different things. Why not try making lots of letters with playdough?

What you need

Playdough (see playdough recipe on page 272)

Letter cards

Preparation

Grab yourself some playdough and a flat surface and you are ready to go!

Activity

Support your child in making and building their own alphabet out of playdough. It is wise to focus on two or three letters each time you do this activity rather than all of them at once. This is a fun way to practise letter formation in a tactile way without pen and paper.

If your child is finding the shape-building difficult, try making the shape for them and prompt them to trace over the letter to practise the formation of the letter.

Letter-writing is a tricky business, but enjoy exploring the different shapes.

Remember

Letters are written a specific way. We always write from left to right and top to bottom. See page 276 for the letter-writing prompts.

m
s

Pre-writing Scribbling

This activity covers Fine Motor Skills. Often children are told not to scribble but I say, let's get scribbling! All of the letters in the alphabet are formed with a series of lines, zigzags, curves and dots. Exploring and drawing these shapes all leads to forming letters.

What you need

A large roll of paper

Pens, crayons or paint sticks

Tape to hold down paper

TOP TIP
We love to use paint sticks for preschoolers because they are easy to hold and glide easily on the paper.

Preparation

Roll out some paper onto a hard floor or a table – the bigger the better. Tape down the edges and grab some paints, pens or crayons.

Activity

Pre-writing shapes and scribbles are a fun way to get your child practising their writing skills. The shapes and patterns do not have to be perfect. The idea is they practise forming different shapes and movements.

The younger your child is, the bigger you want the shapes and patterns to be. Let them express themselves and enjoy the process.

Different types of pen grip

Fisted/palmar grasp In this grasp, the pencil is held in the palm with the fingers wrapped around it.

Quadrupod grasp Using four fingers to hold the pencil for more stability but main movements usually initiated from the wrist.

Tripod grasp In the tripod grasp, the pencil is held between the thumb and index finger, with the middle finger providing support. This is the preferred way to hold a pen/pencil.

To prompt your child to use the tripod grasp try using our 'tweety fingers' method. Use your thumb, index and middle fingers and say 'tweet tweet' like a bird. Then pick up your pencil near the writing end and flip it back. It should sit perfectly in your hand.

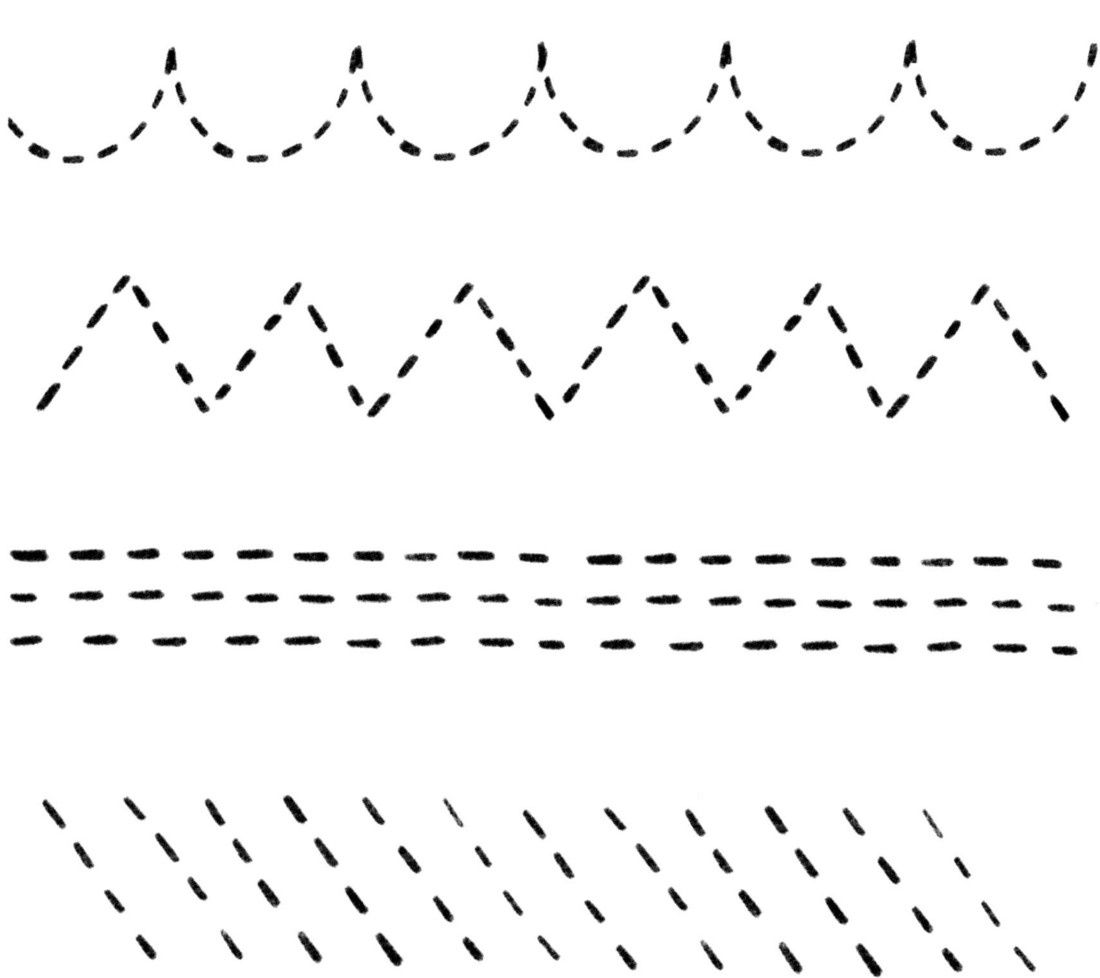

Clap and Stomp

This activity covers Rhythm and Rhyme while looking at syllables. Hearing syllables in words can be difficult but syllables are a very important part of word formation. Try clapping and stomping your way through learning.

What you need

Hands and feet to clap and stomp

Preparation

Find a quiet space and you are ready.

Activity

Syllables are like little beats or chunks in words. When you say a word, you can clap your hands for each beat you hear. Each clap represents one syllable. For example:

'Cat' has one syllable, so you would clap once.
'Dog' also has one syllable, so again you would clap once.
'Table' has two syllables, so you would clap twice: Ta-ble.
'Elephant' has three syllables, so you would clap three times: El-e-phant.

Some words have many syllables, while others have just one or two. Clapping out the syllables can help you understand how to say words correctly and helps with spelling and pronunciation!

IDEA BANK

One syllable	Two syllables	Three syllables
Cat	Table	Elephant
Dog	Window	Chocolate
Book	Rabbit	Umbrella
Sun	Happy	Computer
Run	Funny	Tomato
Hat	Flower	Banana
Bed	Butter	Octopus

Sound Sandwich

This activity covers Alliteration. Who doesn't love a sandwich? Well, these sandwiches are slightly different. They are made of playdough and have a letter filling. They do not sound appetising, but they will definitely help with sound recognition.

What you need

Playdough (see playdough recipe on page 272)

Small objects/magnetic letters

Biscuit cutter

Preparation

Grab some playdough and fill a basket with some small objects. They can be any object or toys that your child loves to play with.

Activity

Using a biscuit cutter, cut out two playdough shapes the same size and hide an object/letter in the middle. Repeat this step as many times as you like. Prompt your child to come and join your sandwich shop. What sandwich will they choose? What is in the middle?

Prompt your child to tell you what's inside and explore the letter/initial sound of that object.

Why not let your child open up their own sandwich shop and let you choose?

Follow the Leader

This activity covers Body Percussion. We can make so many different sounds using our bodies. Body percussion is a fun way to explore the ways our bodies can move and to enhance our coordination and rhythmic skills.

What you need

A large, quiet space

Preparation

No preparation is needed for this activity.

Activity

Body percussion involves using parts of the body to create sounds and rhythms. Explore moving and making sounds and getting your child to copy you. This is called Follow the Leader, so give your child some examples but then let them become the leader.

- Clapping hands together to produce a sharp, clear sound.
- Stomping feet on the ground to create a bold, resonant sound.
- Snapping fingers to produce a fast-paced clicking sound.
- Patting thighs with hands to create a deep, rhythmic sound.
- Tapping or drumming on the chest with hands to produce a hollow sound.
- Gently tapping cheeks with fingers to create a popping sound.
- Tapping fingers on a hard surface, like a table, to produce a light, rhythmic sound.
- Making sounds with the mouth, like clicks, pops or 'beatboxing' effects.
- Rubbing hands together to produce a soft, swishing sound.
- Clapping hands behind the back for a different acoustic effect.

Pat
Click
Stomp

Rhyming Word Snap

This activity covers Rhythm and Rhyme. Have you ever heard of the game Snap? This is just like that, but you must close your eyes and listen for the rhyming words. Shout 'snap' when you hear them!

What you need

All you need is a quiet space to complete this activity

Preparation

No preparation is needed for this activity.

Activity 1

Recognising and producing rhyming words helps children break down and manipulate sounds in words.

Practise saying some rhyming words with your child by saying, 'What rhymes with cat? Mat or dog?' This will build their confidence and understanding which will then lead into being able to play Snap.

Activity 2 – Snap

Say a list of random words and embed some rhyming words in the list. Prompt your child to shout 'SNAP!' when they hear the rhyming words.

IDEA BANK

cat – hat	fish – dish	pan – man
dog – frog	ball – tall	bat – rat
sun – fun	fox – box	toy – boy
car – star	duck – truck	hill – bill
pig – wig	bed – red	light – kite
tree – bee	mug – bug	pen – hen
	cup – pup	
	mouse – house	

Word Family Blocks

This activity covers Oral Blending and Segmenting. Did you know that words belong to families? Just like we have a family, so do some words. Let's look at some word families together and explore how they change.

What you need

Building blocks (Mega Bloks and Duplo are best for this activity)

Dry erase markers

Preparation

Grab some plastic building blocks and write letters on them with a dry erase marker. Write consonants on single bricks and word families such as at, am, en, in, ig, op, un and on double bricks.

Activity

Word families share similar letter combinations and typically have the same ending, which helps with spelling and pronunciation.

Explore the different word families together by adding a consonant brick to the start of the word, and listening to the way it changes every time you change the initial sound brick. This makes sounding and blending words much simpler as the word ending stays the same.

IDEA BANK

at	an	en	in	ip	op	un
bat	man	den	bin	chip	bop	bun
cat	pan	hen	fin	dip	chop	fun
chat	plan	men	kin	drip	cop	gun
fat	can	pen	pin	flip	crop	nun
flat	fan	ten	shin	grip	drop	pun
hat	ran	then	skin	hip	flop	run
mat	clan	when	spin	lip	hop	shun
pat	bran		thin	ship	lop	spun
rat	ban		sin	sip	mop	stun
sat			win	skip	plop	sun
spat			twin	slip	pop	

bat
c
r
f

Blend Around the House

This activity covers Oral Blending and Segmenting. Blending can be tricky! That's why blending around the house is a brilliant tool for children, it helps to provide a context and gives children a deeper understanding of what blending is!

What you need

All you need is a few simple phrases, and you can introduce this activity to your everyday learning

Preparation

No preparation is needed for this activity.

Activity

Teaching a preschooler to blend sounds into words is a crucial step in developing early reading skills. Blending involves combining individual sounds to form words; in this activity we will be looking at orally blending the sounds in words.

It is a very simple game, like I spy but instead of guessing the object, children blend the word at the end of the sentence. Here are a few examples for you to try:

'Can you pass me the red c-u-p?'
'Where is Mummy's m-u-g?'
'Let's go up to b-e-d!'
'Can you see the yellow v-a-n?'
'I would like to play with the b-r-i-ck-s'

You can make the end word more and more complex as your child begins to orally blend the sounds together. By incorporating this skill into your daily routine, your child will build their confidence around blending.

Note
This activity can be completed anywhere – not just in the house! We often play this game in the car.

Sound and Match

This activity covers Oral Blending and Segmenting. Let's play a game of matching. Listen closely and find the picture that matches the word. It's as simple as that!

What you need

A selection of pictures of CVC words

Preparation

Draw or print pictures of simple CVC words.

Activity

Simple CVC words are great for beginner readers because all the words contain their short vowel sound and are the simplest words to blend and segment.

Simply choose a word to blend aloud for your child to find, for example b-u-s. Repeat until your child has found all of the correct pictures.

Once your child can confidently blend the sounds and match each of the objects, prompt them to segment the sounds in words. For example, pick up the picture of the bus and explain that the word bus has three sounds. Which three sounds can your child hear? Work together to hear each of the three sounds together.

Remember

Blending is for reading: when you smoothly join the sounds together to form a word.

Segmenting is for spelling: when you break a word up and separate the sounds in a word.

IDEA BANK

a	e	i	o	u
cat	bed	fig	dog	bug
hat	red	pig	log	jug
mat	hen	kid	hog	mug
rat	pen	bin	mop	rug
fan	ten	pin	pot	sun
van	leg	tin	cot	bun
pan	peg	lip	rod	nut
map	net	zip	pod	cup

AGE
4–5

PHASE 2

Phase 2 phonics is typically taught to children during their first year of school, around the ages of four to five. This phase covers nineteen letters of the alphabet, and its main goal is to teach children the basic sounds that letters make. This enables them to begin blending the sounds to read simple words and segment them to spell.

If you find yourself in this chapter of the book and your child has not yet started school, explore the sounds at your own leisure. Take your time to look at the letters. Explore two sounds per week in lots of detail. Look at how they are formed and what sounds they make.

Most importantly, enjoy the explorative nature of phonics.

Phonics is best taught alongside lots of gross and fine motor activities.

Scan QR code for an optional resource shortcut!

Phase 2 looks at four main aspects

Letters and Sounds

Learning and exploring nineteen letters of the alphabet, their names and the sounds that they make.

Blending Skills

Developing children's ability to blend sounds together to read simple words.

Segmenting Skills

Developing children's ability to segment words into individual sounds to spell and write them.

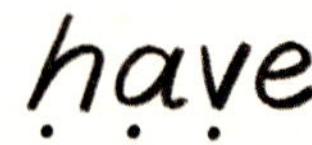

Sight Words

Learning and exploring a series of high-frequency words and how to read them by sight.

Important information

- It is important to ensure you are articulating each sound correctly: this is called the 'pure sound'. It is very common for children (and some adults) to add a 'schwa' to the end of some sounds.
- The 'schwa' is often added to the end of sounds – it sounds like an 'uh' so instead of ssss you might hear some people say 'suh'. It is important NOT to add a schwa because it makes sounding and blending more challenging.
- Each sound requires one mouth movement. To ensure you are forming the sounds correctly, please see page 278 for our articulation checker. If in doubt, find our videos on YouTube: just search for 'Little Happy Learners'.

The Nineteen Letters

Here are the nineteen letters covered in Phase 2: **s**, **a**, **t**, **p**, **i**, **n**, **m**, **d**, **g**, **o**, **c**, **k**, **e**, **u**, **r**, **h**, **b**, **f** and **l**.

It also covers some consonant digraphs such as **ck**, **ll**, **ss** and **ff**.

The letters are taught in this specific order to ensure that children can begin practising their sounding and blending skills quickly. If you were to teach the letters in alphabetical order, you would need to learn more than nine letters before you could begin to sound and blend simple three letter words.

In education settings, children are typically taught four sounds per week. Between Monday and Thursday, they will learn one sound per day and Fridays are a day to consolidate their learning.

Typical Structure

Week	Sounds covered
1	s, a, t, p
2	i, n, m, d
3	g, o, c, k
4	ck, e, u, r
5	h, b, f, ff
6	l, ll, ss

Sound by Sound

When looking at each of the letters and sounds in Phase 2, there are lots of elements to consider. For your child to be able to successfully apply their knowledge of each sound to their reading and writing, they should explore the sounds in the following ways:

Letter Name

When introducing the letter and its corresponding sound, begin by telling your child the letter name. For example, you could say, 'This is the letter a (ay) and it makes the sound **ah**.'

Sound Recognition

Knowing the sound is the most important part of Phase 2 phonics, so after introducing the name of the letter, we then put the emphasis on the sound. Each letter has its own unique sound and it is important that children explore the sound multiple times. (Try using a mirror when learning each sound: this supports your children in understanding where their tongue, lips and teeth should be with each sound our mouth makes.) See if you are making the correct mouth shape by checking our Speech Sound Description on page 278.

Initial Sounds in Words

Once your child has explored the sound that each letter makes, try looking at some words that begin with that sound. This helps them to understand that words are made up of different sounds.

Blending

Now you can begin to blend the sounds together to make words. You can begin doing this orally for your child, then work together to recognise the sounds in simple words and blend them together independently. Begin small and work your way up. For example: **i-n** (in); **i-n-k** (ink); **p-i-n** (pin).

Letter Formation

Ensuring that children form the letters correctly, right from the very beginning, is extremely important. Letters should be written from top to bottom and left to right. Please find the letter-writing prompts on page 276, which explain how each of the letters should be formed. (If formed correctly from the beginning, children will find it easier to write with cursive handwriting later.)

Segmenting/Chopping It Up

Segmenting for spelling is a similar process to blending but the children hear the word first. For example, to spell the word cat your child will need to chop the word up into three separate sounds: **c-a-t**. You can support your child with this skill by telling them how many sounds are in the word and by repeating the word several times to highlight the beginning, middle and end sounds.

Sounds and Actions

We have always found it useful to introduce each sound with an action. It makes the process engaging and helps children to commit the sound to memory. Find our list of actions on page 274.

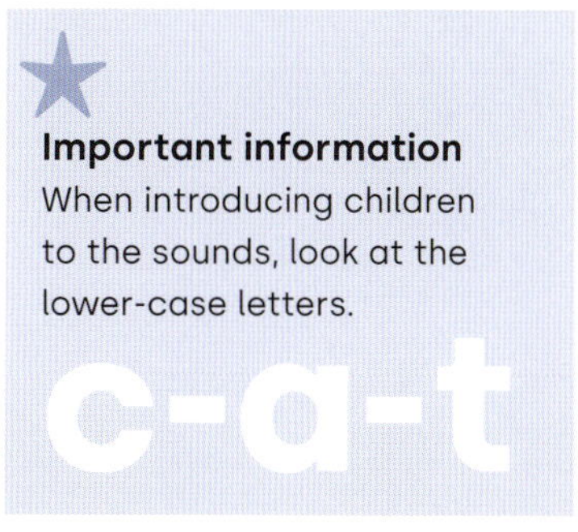

Sight Words

In Phase 2, children are introduced to five new sight words. Sight words (also known as high-frequency words) are words that do not follow phonetic rules. So, children need to learn them by sight and learn to 'crack the code'. This is a term that I use regularly in phonics, because not all words follow the rules and we often need to look at a word in more detail to be able remember it.

For example, the word 'no' cannot be sounded out but if we explore the word in more detail, the **o** is making its vowel sound (also known as its long sound), so it reads **n-oh**. This is the same for the word 'go'.

However, it is not the case for the word 'to'. In the word 'to', the **o** is making an **oo** sound. So, the best way to explore this with your child is by learning by sight or creating fun ways to remember.

Here are the five sight words covered in Phase 2:
the, **no**, **go**, **I**, **to**

In this chapter you will find eighteen different activities to complete with your child: they cover all aspects of Phase 2 phonics and are designed to be enjoyed multiple times with each of the sounds.

Take your time and enjoy the process. Phonics should be

Contents

TOP TIPS

Try providing your child with a handheld mirror so they can watch the way their mouth moves as they voice the sounds.

Keep sessions at home short and fun – five to ten minutes is enough!

Bathtime is a fun way to get some phonics into your day: grab yourself some foam letters (make sure they are lower case) and get recognising sounds and spelling words in the bath.

This chapter has been designed for children between the ages of four and five, but that is not to say younger children cannot enjoy it too. Explore the sounds at your own pace: you know your child best and when they are ready to embark on their phonics journey. If your child is showing interest in reading and can sit at an activity for five minutes, they may be ready for more.

Playdough Prints

This activity focuses on Spelling. Printing can be fun and it takes the pressure off children because they do not need to focus on their letter formation: they can focus solely on sound recognition and blending or spelling.

What you need

Playdough (see playdough recipe on page 272)

Magnetic letters

Remember

Some sounds are *stretchy* and some are *bouncy*.

Stretchy sounds are pronounced in one continuous sound. Try stretching it as long as you can, for example '**Mmmmmm**onkey'. **M**, **f**, **l**, **n**, **r**, **s**, **v** and **z** are all stretchy sounds.

Bouncy sounds are said with a short, sharp gap in between each repetition, for example **d-d-d**og. **D**, **b**, **c**, **k**, **g**, **h**, **j**, **p**, **qu**, **t**, **w**, **x**, **y**, and the vowels **a**, **e**, **i**, **o**, and **u** are all bouncy sounds.

Preparation

Gather what you need and find a quiet space. Set up your space with consonants on one side and vowels on the other. This will help when forming some simple CVC words.

Activity 1

Roll out a large piece of playdough and ensure that it is smooth and flat. Prompt your child to make some simple prints into the dough. Begin by naming the letters and exploring their sounds. Is the letter a vowel or a consonant? Is it a bouncy sound or a stretchy sound? What do you know about the letter?

Activity 2

Prompt your child to form some simple CVC words, tell them a word and get them to chop the word up to spell. Say the word aloud and count the sounds together. Support your child to find the correct letters. Draw your child's attention to the fact that the vowel always goes in the middle of CVC words.

IDEA BANK

a	e	i	o	u
pat	jet	bit	hot	sum
cab	pet	rid	mob	cup
tan	beg	wig	fog	nut
rag	fed	him	cop	fun
ham	yet	zip	job	hug

pen
pen

Sensory Shapes

This activity focuses on Writing. Multi-sensory play is motivating and engaging for young children and has been proven to help children to retain information and to stay focused for longer periods of time.

What you need

A tray

Oobleck

A craft stick

Letter cards

How to make Oobleck

Oobleck is very easy to make. You just need cornflour and water. Use the ratio 2:1 and you cannot go wrong. Two cups of cornflour and one cup of water. Feel free to add some food colouring to make it vibrant and fun.

Preparation

Prepare a tray with the Oobleck mix. Provide your child with a set of letter cards to copy.

Activity

Oobleck is a fantastic sensory base to explore, especially when writing letters! Give it a go by using a craft stick or your finger to form a letter in the Oobleck base. You must be quick before the letter vanishes before your eyes.

This is the perfect way to explore letter-writing: there is no right or wrong way and it is super fun!

Oobleck

Oobleck is a non-Newtonian liquid made from a mix of cornstarch and water. It acts like a liquid when at rest and like a solid when put under pressure.

Invisible Writing

This activity focuses on Blending and Sight Words. Unleash your inner magician with this wonderful magic trick. It is guaranteed to impress any child, but make sure it is a surprise!

What you need

White crayon or a white candle

Paper

Watercolour paints or food colouring and water

Paintbrush

Preparation

Write a series of letters, CVC words or sight words on a piece of paper using a white crayon.
(Do this without your child seeing so that it looks like magic.)

Activity

Provide your child with some watercolours and a paintbrush. Prompt them to paint over the paper to reveal the invisible writing. What sounds can they identify? Can they blend the sounds in simple CVC words? Can they recall some of the Phase 2 sight words?

TOP TIPS

For many activities you will be using CVC words, so it is important to look at the difference between consonants and vowels. Try singing along (to the tune of *Old Macdonald*) to our vowel song, which goes like this:

There are some letters you should know,
And vowels are their name-o.
A, E, I, O, U
A, E, I, O, U
A, E, I, O, U
And vowels are their name-o.

For the whole song turn to page 283.

dog
hen

Cup Families

This activity focuses on Blending. Twisty cups can be used again and again, and are a fantastic way to explore word families!

What you need

Paper cups

Pens

Preparation

Create twisty cups by cutting a small rectangular window out of one cup. Next to the window write one of the word family endings, for example 'en'.

On a second cup, write a series of consonants around the centre. (These consonants should be positioned at the same level as the window.) Place the first cup on top of the second cup and twist. As you twist, one consonant should show through the window at a time.

Activity

Provide your child with a selection of twisty cups. Prompt them to twist the cups to change the words each time. Help them to blend the word ending and then hear how it changes each time they twist the cup.

IDEA BANK

at	an	en	in	ip	op	un
bat	man	den	bin	hip	bop	bun
cat	pan	hen	fin	lip	cop	fun
fat	can	men	tin	dip	hop	pun
hat	fan	pen	pin	sip	lop	run
mat	ran	ten	win	rip	mop	sun

Word families are groups of words that follow the same phonetic pattern (usually at the end of the word). Looking at word families helps children with blending because they only focus on changing the initial sounds!

chat
top

Tube Drops

This activity focuses on Sound Recognition. Ball drops and marble runs can provide hours of fun, so let's make a letter drop.

What you need

Cardboard tubes

Pens

Pompoms

Dot stickers

Preparation

Tape cardboard tubes to your window or wall.

Write a different letter on each of the cardboard tubes. Use as many tubes as you like. On a series of dot stickers write the same letters multiple times. Put a letter sticker on each pompom.

Activity

Prompt your child to sort the pompoms by placing them into the correct cardboard tubes.

Watch as your child sorts the letters, then prompt them to name each letter and tell you the sound it makes and some words that begin with that sound.

a
p
i
n

Word Makers

This activity focuses on Blending. Word makers are a fun way to practise blending skills. How many words can you make on one word maker?

What you need

A piece of paper or cardboard

Post-it notes

Pen

Glue stick

Preparation

Cut a piece of paper or cardboard so that it fits three Post-it notes side by side.

Activity

Prompt your child to think of a simple CVC word. For example, cat. Segment the sounds in the word and write each of the letters on a Post-it note, one letter per Post-it.

Stick each of the Post-it notes onto the cardboard.

Now encourage your child to think about all the words that rhyme with your chosen word. If you are using 'cat', for example, these words belong to the 'at' family.

Ask your child to change the word into a new word by sticking a new sound over the first letter. If you are using 'cat' as your word, stick a new sound over the letter c. How many times can they change the word?

You can make as many word makers as you want. They are a brilliant resource to practise blending skills.

Reminder

When segmenting for a CVC word, make sure to count the sounds in the word first and talk about the beginning, middle and end sounds.

Say it, Make it, Write it!

This activity focuses on Sight Words. It is a multi-sensory approach to spelling. Say the word aloud, make it with magnetic letters and then write it.

What you need

A whiteboard

Dry erase marker

Magnetic letters

Preparation

No preparation is needed for this activity.

Activity

This activity requires your child to read a word, then make it with magnetic letters or build it with bricks and then write it themself. It is a multi-faceted activity where reading and spelling skills can be practised together.

Once your child has finished each step, cover it up so that they do not just copy.

You can do this activity with sight words or CVC words.

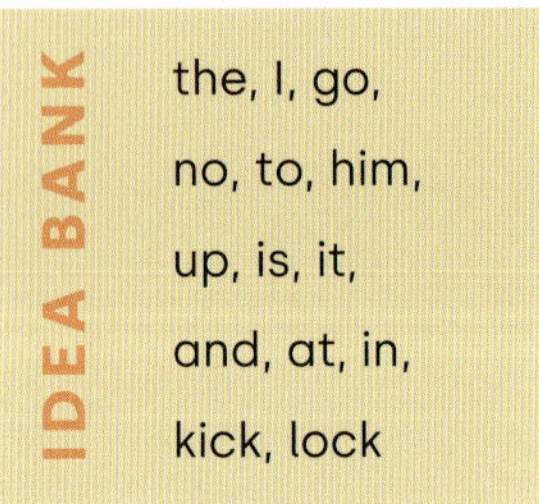

the

t h e

the

Word Towers

This activity focuses on Spelling. Building words with blocks is a great way to practise spelling skills. Name the picture and spell the CVC word.

What you need

Pictures of simple CVC words

Mega Bloks, Duplo or building blocks

Dry erase marker or masking tape and pen

Preparation

Print or draw some simple CVC objects. Write a series of letters on the building blocks with a dry erase marker. If you are using masking tape and a pen, write onto the tape then stick onto single blocks.

Separate the blocks into vowels and consonants to make the activity a little simpler.

Activity

Prompt your child to spell the words and then label the pictures by using the building blocks. As always when segmenting, make sure you count the sounds and then work out each sound individually.

As you go, discuss where you find the vowel in each of the words.

IDEA BANK

cat	star
duck	cup
dog	pig
bed	rat
sun	fox
bug	hen

CVC Words

A CVC word is a simple word that follows the pattern of consonant, vowel, consonant.

Try exploring vowels and consonants together. Which letters are vowels? Make up a rhyme or song with your child to help them to remember the special vowels.

p
i
d
u
ck
a
g
t

Blending Bus

This activity focuses on Blending. Use a toy car or bus to drive under a CVC word to support the blending for reading process.

What you need

A toy car or bus, or a toy of your choice

A paper or cardboard 'road'

Letter cards

Preparation

Make a small road with paper or cardboard and write some sounds on the cards.

Activity

Using the cards, form a three-letter word above the road. Prompt your child to drive/walk their car/bus/toy along the road. As the bus/toy passes each sound, prompt your child to say the sound aloud.

Drive your car faster and faster until your child can hear the three sounds coming together to form the word.

IDEA BANK

a	e	i	o	u
van	den	bib	pod	mud
map	peg	fit	box	bun
pad	vet	hip	got	nut
wag	men	kid	sob	cub
tap	net	dip	rod	bug

This activity is called the Blending Bus but you can use whatever your child loves the most. The idea is that the 'bus' drives under each sound in a word to help you to read it, but if your child loves a special bear, make the bear walk under each sound to help them instead.

Word of the Day

This activity focuses on Sight Words. Explore a new word of the day each day. Look at a different sight word each day and explore the way it is spelled together.

What you need

White board

Dry erase marker

Word list

Preparation

Find the perfect time of day to introduce a new word to your child.

Activity

Each day, introduce your child to a new word. Look at the way the word is spelled, what letters are in the word and how you can use the word in a sentence.

This is a brilliant way to explore sight words. Sight words are tricky because they do not follow typical phonetic rules. Create your own mnemonics for irregularly spelled words. Mnemonics are memory aids that associate a word with something memorable. For instance, you could create a silly sentence or image to help remember the spelling. These must be memorable to you and your child.

Phase 2 only has five sight words, so for this activity you will find all of the sight words from phases 2 and 3.

PHASE 2&3 SIGHT WORD LIST

a, to, on,
mum, in, at,
with, you,
them, they,
an, if, off, into,
my, then, was,
this, his, I, had,
it, got, we, he,
be, me, go,

back, can, of,
get, that, too,
she, look, dad,
him, big, no,
and, for, her,
down, are, up,
as, but, not,
will, see, now,
all

you
you
y ou → oo

Sight Word Splat

This activity focuses on Sight Words. It's exciting, a little messy and educational. Write sight words on the windows and give your child a spray bottle to splat the correct word.

What you need

Spray bottle

Paint sticks or dry erase marker

Preparation

Using a dry erase marker or paint sticks, write a series of sight words on the windows.

Fill a refillable spray bottle with water.

Activity

Say a sight word aloud and prompt your child to spray the correct word. This is working on their quick and speedy recall skills while letting them get a little messy.

Start this activity with five or six words at a time and build your way up to having a whole window of words.

When your child is confident with sight words, let them practise spelling the words and writing on the windows themselves.

This activity is an amazing way for your child to practise reading skills alongside working their fine motor skills. Give those hand muscles a workout.

Important information

Working on a window offers several benefits for children. When they engage in activities on a vertical surface, they move around and use their whole body. They learn to cross the midline – the imaginary line down the centre of the body that divides it into left and right. It puts the wrist in an extended position, which improves pencil grip, and it is ideal for children who find sitting at a task challenging by sustaining their attention and engaging them in learning more effectively.

I
the
go
to
and

Full Circle

This activity focuses on Segmenting. A game of new words, made from old. You begin and end with the same word and change only a letter or two at a time.

What you need

White board

Dry erase marker

Preparation

No preparation is needed for this activity.

Activity

Tell your chid that today you are going to play a game of Full Circle.

You will say a word and your child will write it on their board. You will then read the next word in the list and your child will have to work out what sound they need to change in the existing word. So, if the first word is 'fat' and the second word is 'pat', they only need to change the initial sound.

Continue down the list until you come back 'Full Circle'.

This is a brilliant way for children to explore words and how they are formed, to look at the sounds in words and learn how words all follow similar patterns.

IDEA BANK

fat	cat	bus	fit	hen	jet	hot
pat	bat	bun	pit	men	vet	rot
cat	bag	fun	pat	met	vat	rat
can	bog	fan	pan	pet	van	ram
pan	cog	fat	fan	pit	pan	ham
fan	cot	bat	fat	pin	pat	hat
fat	cat	but	fit	pen	pet	hot
		bus		hen	jet	

bus
bun
fun
fat
fan

Web Writing

This activity focuses on Segmenting. It is a simple game of spelling without writing a single letter. Let's make a spider's web together.

What you need

Paper

Pencil or pen

Preparation

Draw a large circle on a piece of paper. Around the circle write a series of letters, ensuring that you have more than one vowel. (You can plan this activity to look at one sound at a time.)

Activity

Say a word aloud and prompt your child to draw a line from one sound to another to form the word. Each word on the list will have three lines, so after each of the words has been spelled and joined together you will have a giant spider's web of spellings on the page.

This is a pressure-free way of spelling – much better than writing words in a list!

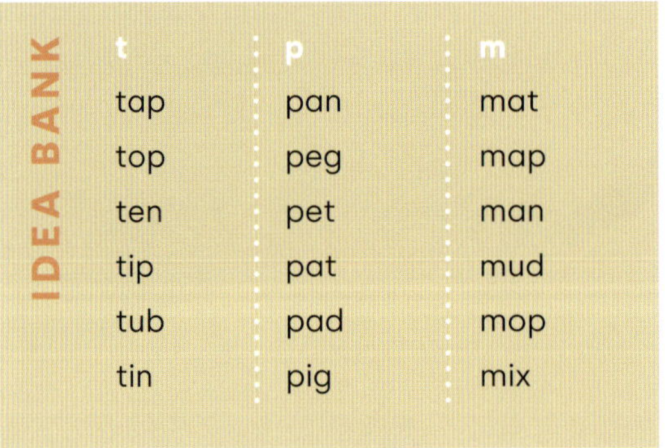

IDEA BANK

t	p	m
tap	pan	mat
top	peg	map
ten	pet	man
tip	pat	mud
tub	pad	mop
tin	pig	mix

p
t
n
u
s
i
m
o

Craft-stick Finger Spacers

This activity focuses on Sentence Structure. Sometimes you just need something to help you to remember your finger spaces!

What you need

Craft sticks

Felt-tip pens

Glitter, stickers (optional)

Preparation

No preparation is needed for this activity.

Activity

Explain to your child that when you write a sentence you need to remember three key things: capital letters at the beginning of the sentence, finger spaces between each word and a full stop at the end of the sentence. Today, you are going to make your own finger spacer to help you with sentence writing.

Design your finger spacer together, get as creative as possible and let your child make all the decisions. This is to make writing more fun and to give them confidence with their sentence structure.

Give it a go! Ask your child to write a sentence remembering the three key elements. Make sure they use the finger spacer to put a small space in between each of the words.

SIMPLE SENTENCE BANK

A pig in the bin.

A cat can nap.

A big red bus.

The hen can run.

Learning to write sentences can be complex for children and often the thing that they find most difficult is remembering to use finger spaces. Having a simple tool like this to hand acts as a reminder.

I am a kid.

Pompom Buttons

This activity focuses on Blending. When your child needs a little support with blending, add some sound buttons and get pressing!

What you need

Pompoms

White board

Dry erase marker

Preparation

No preparation is needed for this activity.

Activity

Blending can be tricky. When you need to break it down and make it easier for your child to hear, this activity can really help.

Write a word on the white board but leave a large space in-between each of the letters so that you can accentuate each of the sounds.

Place a pompom under each of the sounds. Model how to sound out a word and stretch the central sound. When you say the initial sound, press the pompom like it's a button. When you say the vowel sound, pick up the pompom and drag it while stretching the sound. Then press the last pompom and say the end sound, for example caaaaaaaaat.

This should help your child to hear the sounds and blend them together while having a multi-sensory way of exploring reading. After modelling using the sound buttons, prompt your child to give it a go independently.

z
i
p

Word Prison

This activity focuses on Segmenting. All the words have been locked up but each sound must go into its own cell. Your child needs to split up the sounds in each of the words and LOCK THEM UP!

What you need

Pen

Paper

Magnetic letters

Preparation

Draw a grid with three cells on a piece of paper.

Activity

Explain to your child that all the words on your list have been really naughty and they have been put into Word Prison. Each word needs to be split up because only one sound can go into a cell!

Provide your child with one word at a time. Can they split the sounds up and put them in their own cells? This is a fun spin on segmenting for spelling. You can do this with a group of CVC words or with a list of spellings.

IDEA BANK

ss	ll	ff	zz
mess	dull	cuff	buzz
less	pill	off	fizz
kiss	well	huff	fuzz
boss	will	puff	jazz
fuss	sell	stiff	whizz

You could do this activity with **CVC** words, or you could focus on words with double consonants, like those listed above.

Double consonants like **ss**, **ll**, **ff**, **zz** are children's first introduction to digraphs. A digraph is two letters that make one sound.

So, remember only one sound can go in each cell; **ff**, **ss**, **ll** and **zz** are all one sound!

d
o
t

Letter Detectives

This activity focuses on Sound Recognition. Can your child become a real-life detective and find the missing letters?

What you need

Magnetic letters

Paper

Pen

Preparation

Hide magnetic letters around the house.

Write some CVC words on paper with a sound missing in each of the words.

Activity

Explain to your child that today they are a detective and their very special mission is to find the missing letters. The letters have all gone into hiding around the house and they need to be found.

Look at each of the prepared word cards and prompt your child to read the word and think about what sound is missing.

Hunt around the house for the missing letter. When they have found it, place it on the word card and read the word aloud. Could they have found another letter to make a different word?

Continue until your child has completed each of the word cards.

It's important to remember that there will be more than one correct answer for each of the **CVC** words. Hide more letters than you need so that they can succeed in this mission!

Capital Letter Hop

This activity focuses on Sound Recognition. Some capital letters look completely different from their lower-case form, so why not practise saying the letter name and recognising those trickier capital letters.

What you need

Large pieces of paper/card

Felt tip pens

Preparation

Make your own capital letter cards by writing a large capital letter on a piece of paper for every letter of the alphabet.

Activity

Sing the alphabet song together while showing your child the corresponding letter.

Place some capital letters on the floor and call out a letter name.

Prompt your child to hop like a bunny onto the correct capital letter. (Try using five or six cards at a time.)

Support your child to recall each of the letter names and then hop to the next letter.

Have fun with this gross motor activity. Try adding some rhythm and rhyme to it by singing 'Hop Little Bunnies'.

Let your child have a go at writing some of the capital letters, this will help to support their sentence-writing skills.

TOP TIPS

In Phase 3 your children will begin using the letter names more frequently and will begin to become more confident using capital letters in their sentence writing.

Confidence is gained through practice. Try playing this game alongside a capital and lower-case letter-matching game.

AGE
4–5

PHASE 3

Phase 3 phonics is typically taught to children during their first year of school, around the ages of four to five. This phase covers twenty-five new graphemes and twelve new sight words. In this phase, children are introduced to more complex sounds known as digraphs and trigraphs and they will build upon the foundations laid out in Phases 1 and 2, developing their decoding and blending skills further.

When learning digraphs, it is important to use the letter name rather than the sound. For example, you could introduce the sound and say, 'N (en) and G (gee) come together to make the sound ng as in ring.'

Scan QR code for an optional resource shortcut!

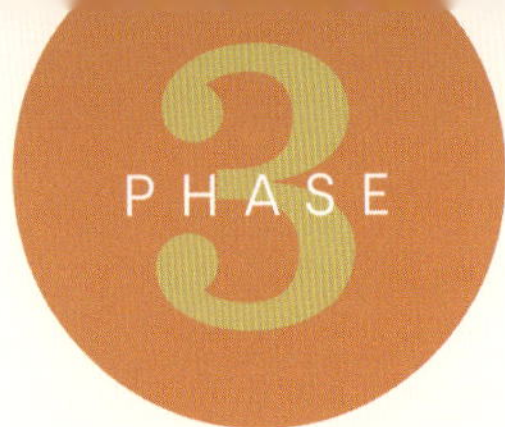

Phase 3 looks at three main aspects

Complex Sounds

In Phase 3, children are introduced to twenty-five new graphemes, including digraphs and trigraphs.

Reading and Spelling

Using the new phonemes, children will practise reading and spelling words, and start to read and write simple sentences.

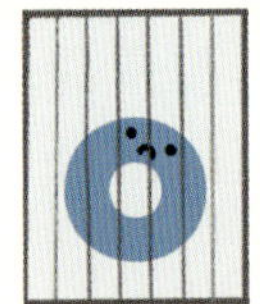

Developing Blending and Segmenting Skills

Children continue to practise blending sounds to read words and segmenting words to spell them.

Important information

Grapheme

A grapheme is the written form of a sound (e.g. s, a): the letter or letters used to represent the sound on paper.

Phoneme

A phoneme is the unit of sound (e.g. **sss**, **ah**). Some phonemes contain more than one letter but only create one sound.

Phase 3 Sounds

Phase 3 includes the remaining letters of the alphabet. These letters are more complex and are used less frequently. Here are the remaining sounds:
j, **v**, **w**, **x**, **ss**, **y**, **z**, **zz**, **qu**.

Consonant Digraphs

A consonant digraph is a combination of two consonants that represent one sound. For example, the 'wr' digraph represents the sound **r** in words like write, wriggle and wrong.

ch – chip
sh – shed
th has a voiced and unvoiced sound – thin/them
ng – ring

Vowel Digraphs

Vowel digraphs are combinations of two vowels that make a single sound.

ai – rain
ee – sleep
oa – goat
oo makes two sounds – book/moon
oi – soil

Digraphs

Digraphs are combinations of two letters, a vowel and consonant, that make a single sound.

ar – barn
or – torn
ur – burn
ow makes two sounds – blow/brown
er – letter

Trigraphs

A trigraph is when three letters come together to make one sound.

igh – night **ear** – fear **air** – hair **ure** – pure

Blending with Complex Sounds

Reading words with complex sounds (sounds with more than one letter) can be a challenge. One way to support children with this is by using dots and dashes.

Using dots and dashes when blending sounds is a helpful technique for teaching phonics, especially in the early stages of reading development. This method is often referred to as 'sound buttons' and is a visual representation of the different sounds in a word.

g oa t sh e d l o ck n igh t

The dots represent single phonemes (individual sounds) and help children see each sound distinctly. The dashes represent digraphs/trigraphs and help children recognise that certain letter combinations produce a single sound.

Reading can be overwhelming for children. Dots and dashes break reading down into manageable parts, reducing cognitive load and making it easier for children to focus on one sound at a time.

Important information
A fun way for children to understand the concept of digraphs and trigraphs is by calling them 'best friends'. I like to explain that the two letters are best friends and when they are together, they make a new sound.

Segmenting with Complex Sounds

Segmenting for spelling is a difficult concept for children to grasp and it can take time to build their confidence. Using a phoneme frame is a practical method for teaching segmenting. Phoneme frames help children visually break down words into their individual sounds.

A phoneme frame is a simple grid that is split into cells. Each cell holds one sound.

Here is an example of a phoneme frame in action.

Phoneme frames help children recognise that certain letter combinations like 'sh' or 'igh' make one sound, which is crucial for mastering the more complex phonics taught in Phase 3.

Sight Words

In Phase 3, children are introduced to fifteen new sight words. Sight words, or high-frequency words, are words that do not follow phonetic rules.

Here are the fifteen sight words covered in Phase 3: **he**, **she**, **we**, **me**, **be**, **was**, **you**, **they**, **all**, **are**, **my**, **her**, **said**, **have**, **like**

Mnemonics are a great way to learn sight words. They help to make information more memorable by creating a link between the sight word and a memorable phrase, image or story, which make children more likely to remember the word.

Here are a few examples:
was – **w**orms **a**re **s**quishy.
all – **a**nts **l**ove **l**eaves.
said – **s**illy **a**nts **i**n **d**resses.

TOP TIP

At this stage it is important for children to know the five vowels because they play an important role in reading and writing complex words.

Try this song:
(to the tune of 'Twinkle Twinkle Little Star')

A, E, I, O, U are vowels,
each one has its special sounds.

Typical Structure

When you begin introducing a new sound, it is good to follow the same structure each time.

Children thrive with structure and routine and love being able to predict what is coming next.

Here is an example structure that we would follow at home when looking at a new sound:

1 Recap previous single sounds. You can do this with letter names or sounds. Do this at a fast pace! We call this 'speed sounds'.

2 Introduce the new sound or the sound of the day. Tell the children the names of the letter(s) and the sound they make.

3 Look at words that contain that sound. For example, if you are looking at the 'oa' digraph you could use the words goat, coat, boat and moat.

4 Read some words containing that sound (boat, goat, float). Remember to add dots and dashes under each of the words for added support.

5 Practise writing the sound in the air, on a white board, in a word or in a sentence. Here is an example sentence: The goat sat in the boat.

In this chapter you will find eighteen activities covering all aspects of Phase 3 phonics and ways you can play repeatedly.

Important information

We have always found it useful to introduce each sound with an action. It makes the process engaging and helps children to commit the sound to memory.
Find our list of actions on page 270.

Contents

TOP TIPS

When introducing complex sounds, remember to teach children to use their fingers to count sounds in words; this will help as a visual aid when sounding and blending.

Use sound buttons (dots under each sound) to help them visually separate and blend sounds in words.

Try to make each session as engaging as possible by adding songs, rhymes and actions.

This chapter has been designed for children between the ages of four and five, during their first year of school. However, every child develops their reading at their own pace so explore the sounds together and follow your own structure and routine. Enjoy the process.

Digraph Flowers

This activity focuses on Sound Recognition. Look closely at the flowers and the words on the petals. Can you make a beautiful digraph bouquet to enjoy?

What you need

Craft sticks

Paper

Glue stick

Preparation

Write three or four digraphs on small circles of paper (one diagraph per circle).

Stick the digraphs onto craft sticks.

Cut six petals for each flower.
Write words containing the chosen digraphs on each of the petals.

Activity

Prompt your child to 'spot the digraph' in the words on the petals and add the petal to the correct flower.

By the end of the activity, you will have a beautiful bouquet of digraph flowers.

By spotting the digraph in the words first, you are encouraging your child to decode the trickiest part of the word before they begin to blend the sounds together. This helps with cognitive load, as it helps them to break the word down slowly.

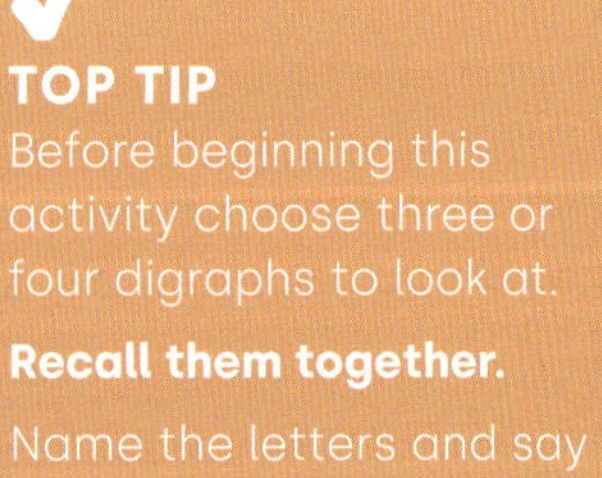

TOP TIP
Before beginning this activity choose three or four digraphs to look at.

Recall them together.

Name the letters and say the sounds aloud.

IDEA BANK

ch	sh	th	ng
chip	ship	thin	ring
chop	shop	think	wing
church	shin	thick	sing
chin	shed	then	thing
chick	fish	them	song
chuck	wish	that	bang

sh
ship
shed

Fishing for Phonics

This activity focuses on Sound Recognition.
Fill a bowl with water, add lots of letters and go fishing.
I wonder what fish you will find inside the water.

What you need

Magnetic letters

Tray

Water

Digraph flashcards

Preparation

Fill a tray with water.

Add letters.

Activity

Looking at one digraph at a time, say the letter names and the sound that they make. Explain that you are going to 'go fishing' and together you are going to make the digraphs.

Prompt your child to find the sounds that belong to each of the digraphs. For example, if you are looking at the 'oa' digraph, your child will need to find an o and an a.

This activity aims to support children in understanding how each of the digraphs are formed.

TOP TIP

Why not try making your own magnetic fishing rod.

Grab yourself a small horseshoe magnet, some twine and two craft sticks.

Tie the magnet to the end of the twine and stick the twine in between the two craft sticks.

IDEA BANK

Try adding some blue food colouring and toy fish to the water; this will engage the children for longer and may even get them playing independently later.

You can purchase digraph magnetic letters if you would like to simplify this activity.

If you do not own magnetic letters, you can make your own 'fish' for this game. Draw the outline of a fish and label it with a letter. Laminate or cover with clear tape (you can use Sellotape or clear packing tape) and add the fish to the water.

Digraph Hunters

This activity focuses on Sound Recognition. You and your child are going on a mission. You have become the Digraph Hunters and it's your job to find all the missing digraphs that are hiding around your house. Where are they and what do they want from you?

What you need

Post-it notes

Pen

Preparation

On a series of Post-it notes, write some words containing digraphs.

Hide the Post-it notes around the house.

Activity

Prompt your child to go on a hunt around the house to find different digraphs.

Provide them with a pen and when they find each of the Post-it notes, ask them to underline the digraph when they spot it. Can they read the word?

Bonus activity

Can your child write some simple sentences containing some of the words?

IDEA BANK

ai	oa	oi	or	ow
rain	boat	foil	torn	cow
fail	toad	coin	fork	brow
ee	**oo**	**ar**	**ur**	**er**
queen	zoom	dart	turn	fern
seem	moon	lark	surf	herd

Note

Spotting the digraph before reading is an important skill for children learning to read.

As children become confident at spotting and reading digraphs, they become more independent and more capable of tackling tricky words on their own.

By identifying digraphs before reading, children can easily recognise the letter combinations and understand that they represent a single sound.

cow
rain

Silly Sentences

This activity focuses on Reading and Spelling. Sentences have never been so fun! Work together to make some silly sentences. You can also focus on sentence formation with this activity.

What you need

Three cups

Craft sticks

Paper and pens

Preparation

Write a series of nouns, verbs and adjectives on a piece of paper.

Cut them out and stick them onto a craft stick.
Sort the sticks into the cups: one cup for nouns, one for verbs and one for adjectives.

Activity

Tell your child to take one stick from each of the cups and make a sentence. They can practise reading the sentences or writing them – it is completely up to you. Enjoy laughing along to some of the strange and silly sentences they create.

Each sentence should start with the word 'the' and follow the pattern: adjective, noun, verb.

Noun

Nouns are words that name people, places or things. For instance:
People: teacher, mum.
Places: school, home.
Things: book, teddy.

Adjective

Adjectives are words that describe the noun. You can use words that describe the colour, shape and size of the noun.

Verb

Verbs are action words. For example, run, jump, swim.

IDEA BANK

adjectives	nouns	verbs
happy big	dog bird	barks flaps
blue green	cat ball	runs rolls
small fast	tree truck	grows honks
red yellow	frog car	jumps waits
tall soft	sun kitten	beams sleeps

SAMPLE SENTENCES

The happy dog barks.
The blue bird flaps.
The small cat runs.
The red ball rolls.
The tall tree grows.
The big truck honks.
The green frog jumps.
The fast car waits.
The yellow sun beams.
The soft kitten sleeps.
When swapped around these sentences become VERY SILLY.

nouns

Crack the Code

This activity focuses on Sight Words. Let's become detectives and take a look at some sight words. Which letters are there to trick us and which ones make their usual sound?

What you need

Sight word flashcards

Highlighter or felt-tip pen

Preparation

Write each of the sight words onto a piece of paper

Cut them out.

Activity

Encourage your child to look at each of the sight words one by one. With each sight word, talk about the sounds that we can hear and the sounds that are trying to 'trick' us.

For example, when looking at the word the – the 'th' is making the correct sound but there is an 'e' on the end that makes no sound at all.

Ask your child to use a highlighter/felt-tip pen to add dots under single sounds and lines under digraphs/trigraphs they can hear. Leave the tricky sounds – this will help them to recall the words when you next look at them.

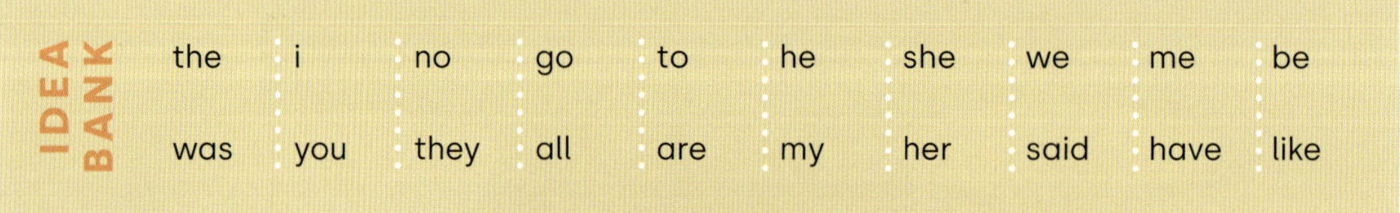

IDEA BANK

the	i	no	go	to	he	she	we	me	be
was	you	they	all	are	my	her	said	have	like

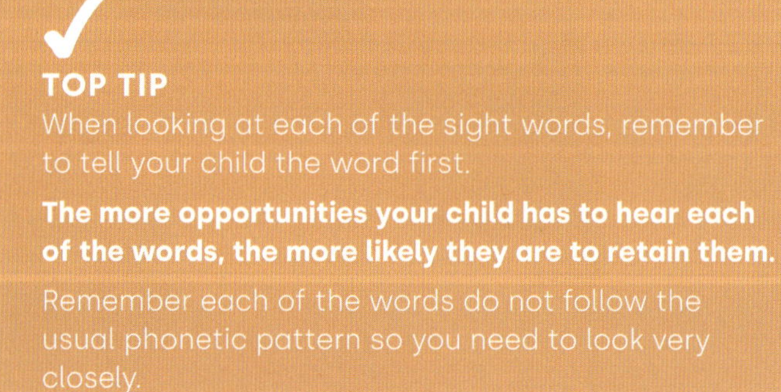

TOP TIP

When looking at each of the sight words, remember to tell your child the word first.

The more opportunities your child has to hear each of the words, the more likely they are to retain them.

Remember each of the words do not follow the usual phonetic pattern so you need to look very closely.

have

The Alphabet

This activity focuses on Letter Recall. Get on board the alphabet train; let's put the letters in alphabetical order!

Preparation

Roll out a large piece of paper on the floor.

Draw a train by creating a series of boxes for each of the letters to fit into.

Write each of the letters of the alphabet on a Post-it note

What you need

A large roll of paper

Pens or paint sticks

Post-it notes

Activity

Prompt your child to order the letters of the alphabet by finding the correct letter on the Post-it notes and add them onto the train.

To add an extra challenge to this activity, you could have each capital letter on one Post-it note and each lower-case letter on another.

TOP TIP

It sounds obvious, but the alphabet song comes in very handy when you are ordering the letters in the alphabet.

It is very common for children to get lost around L M N O P – so take it very slowly.

If your child is confident with ordering the lower-case letters, give capital letters a go!

Tube Puzzles

This activity focuses on Segmenting. Have you ever made a tube puzzle? These stacking puzzles make sounding out so much fun.

What you need

Cardboard tubes (kitchen-roll tubes are ideal)

Pens

Kitchen-roll holder (optional)

Preparation

Grab some cardboard tubes and cut them up into three-centimetre pieces.

Write sounds on the tubes, remembering to include some digraphs and trigraphs.

Activity

This activity focuses on segmenting for spelling. Choose a word and prompt your child to count the sounds in the word, find the sounds they need and then stack them up on top of each other.

It is as simple as that!

TOP TIPS

Start saving your cardboard tubes anytime you get them.

If you don't have any to hand you can easily make your own with a cereal box or paper. Just roll it up and tape along the seam.

To make them reuseable, add some clear packing tape to the outside of the tube before you cut them. You can then write on them with a dry erase marker and use them again and again.

IDEA BANK

ai	oi	ear	oo	oo	igh	air	ure	ee	or
rain	coin	hear	*(long)*	*(short)*	night	hair	pure	see	for
tail	join	fear	moon	book	high	chair	sure	tree	corn
paint	boil	near	food	look	light	fair	cure	bee	born
sail	soil	dear	zoo	foot	right	stair	secure	green	storm
			spoon	cook					

c
o
i
n
p
a
i
n
t
n
e
a
h
l

Sort the Sticks

This activity focuses on Sound Recognition. Sort the sticks into their correct cups. Can you beat the clock?

What you need

Ten cups

Craft sticks

Pen

Preparation

Write some words containing different digraphs on sticks.

Label cups with the digraphs.

Mix up all the sticks and lay them out on a table with the cups on display.

Activity

Prompt your child to read the words on the sticks and place each stick in the correct cup. This is a great activity for focusing on the sounds in words and practising blending skills.

TOP TIP
Once you have made this activity you can play it again and again.
Try leaving it set up for your child to find and they may even practise independently.

IDEA BANK

ch	sh	th UNVOICED	th VOICED	ng	ai	ee	igh	oa	oo LONG
cheese	shell	think	them	king	train	tree	high	goat	moon
chop	sheep	thin	those	song	main	bee	light	boat	food
chest	shine	thumb	mother	wing	wait	see	night	road	spoon
check	shop	thorn	father	long	rain	green	right	coat	zoo
chin	shark	bath	this	ring	paint	feet	bright	float	soon
bench	brush	path	that	bang	snail	sleep	fight	soap	boot
march	crash	moth	brother	string	chain	cheese	sight	loaf	room

spoon
goat
boat
moon
food
see
tree
oa
oo
ee

Pompom Bingo

This activity focuses on Blending. Have a go at playing a game of bingo. What sound can you hear in the word?

What you need

Bingo board

Pompoms

Preparation

Make a bingo board with nine different sounds.

Activity

Say a word from the idea bank aloud and prompt your child to listen closely. What sounds can they hear in the word? This is great for working on their segmenting skills.

Focus on counting the sounds first. For example, mature has four sounds: **m**, **a**, **t**, **ure**. Prompt your child to hold up four fingers and isolate each sound by touching their fingers and saying the sound.

What digraph/trigraph is in the word? Ask your child to place a pompom on the correct sound. Can they get a full board?

IDEA BANK

ar	or	ur	ow	oi	ear	air	ure	er
star	fork	fur	cow	coin	ear	hair	pure	her
car	sort	burn	now	soil	near	chair	sure	term
farm	horn	turn	down	join	fear	fair	cure	verb
park	short	hurt	town	boil	hear	pair	secure	sister
hard	storm	curl	owl	foil	dear	stair	mature	better
garden	sport	surf	brown	oil	year	air	endure	farmer
start	born	church	clown	noise	tear	flair	insure	letter

ar
ear
ure
or
er
ur
ow

Word Walls

This activity focuses on Reading and Blending. Build a sight word brick wall together. With every word you read, the wall gets higher.

What you need

Bricks

A dry erase marker or permanent marker

Preparation

Write sight words on the bricks (one word per brick).

Activity

Prompt your child to read the words displayed on the bricks. With every brick they read, they can begin to build their wall.

Once the wall has been built, it is time to keep it standing.

Say one of the words aloud and ask your child to very gently remove the brick. Can they keep the wall standing without all the words crashing to the ground?

TOP TIP

The best type of bricks to use for this game are Jenga bricks – they work well to encourage independent play after the initial activity. We have a sight word set that we wrote on with permanent marker. It's played with over and over again.

However, you can use whatever bricks you have at home, or even cardboard boxes to make a GIANT wall.

IDEA BANK

Here are more of the most commonly used words

a, about, all, an, and, are, as, at, be, been, but, by, can, come, could, day, did, do, down, each, find, first, for, from, get, go, had, has, have, he, her, him, his, how, I, if, in, is, it, just, like, long, look, made, make, many, me, more, my, no

in
and
find
can
it
is
has
he
if
all
be
how
did
about
make
do
look
him
a
her
could

Sight Word Scramble

This activity focuses on Reading and Blending. Can your child unscramble the letters in a word to spell the word correctly?

What you need

Cups

Magnetic letters

Preparation

Choose ten words from the idea bank below.

Using magnetic letters, make the sight words and place the letters of each word in a separate cup.

Activity

Place your hand on top of the cup and give the cup a little shake.

Throw the letters onto the table and ask your child to arrange the letters so that they correctly spell the sight word.

Challenge your child by letting them explore the letters and see what words they can create.

You can also tell them the sight word that you would like them to spell and watch them arrange them correctly.

TOP TIP

You can play this game with any words, not just sight words.

If you do not have magnetic letters or would like to play this game 'on the go', try writing the words on paper and cutting them up (so that one sound is on each piece of paper), then watch as your child rearranges the letters to spell them correctly.

IDEA BANK

Here are more of the most commonly used words

not, now, of, one, or, other, out, over, said, see, she, so, some, than, that, the, their, them, then, there, these, they, this, time, to, two, up, use, was, water, way, we, were, what, when, which, who, will, with, words, would, write, yes, you, your

t
a
h
t

Syllable Slide

This activity focuses on Blending. Have you ever heard of the syllable slide? It is a little like the 'cha cha slide' but we focus on clapping and sliding whilst learning about syllables.

What you need

Post-it notes

Pen

Preparation

Write some words on Post-it notes, with one syllable on each Post-it. For example, cat has one syllable so therefore would be written on one Post-it note. Tiger has two syllables so therefore would be written on two Post-it notes, as **ti** and **ger**.

Activity

Begin by learning to clap your hands each time you hear a vowel sound or a beat in a word. For example, clap once for cat and twice for tiger.

Look at the words one at a time. Discussing how many syllables you can see and hear.

Muddle up the Post-it notes and prompt your child to slide the syllables together to make all of the two-syllable words.

TOP TIP

A syllable is a part of a word that contains a vowel sound. It's a single, unbroken sound of a word.

Try singing along to our Syllable Slide song:

(Clap your hands)

All right now, we're gonna do the Syllable Slide!
Let's go to work!
To the left, two syllables.
(adult says the word: ti-ger/child claps twice)
Take it back, one syllable.
(adult says the word: cat/ child claps once)

The full song can be found on page 282.

IDEA BANK

One syllable	Two syllables	Three syllables
cat	apple (ap-ple)	elephant (el-e-phant)
dog	baby (ba-by)	chocolate (choc-o-late)
hat	tiger (ti-ger)	dinosaur (di-no-saur)
sun	dinner (din-ner)	butterfly (but-ter-fly)
fish	window (win-dow)	tomato (to-ma-to)
ball	pillow (pil-low)	family (fam-i-ly)

win
dow

Trigraph Roll and Read

This activity focuses on Segmenting. Make a set of dice using a cardboard tube and write the trigraphs **igh**, **ure**, **air** and **ear** on four of the sides. Roll and write!

Preparation

Make the DIY dice.

Write the trigraphs **igh**, **ure**, **air** and **ear** on the faces of one of the dice. On the other die write the numbers one to six.

What you need

Cardboard tubes

Scissors

Pens

Dry erase marker

White board

Activity

Roll the dice. Whatever sound you land on, you must write a word containing that sound. Whatever number you land on, you must write that number of words.

If the sound die lands on a blank face, you can choose a sight word for your child to write.

Your child should write the word on their white board.

How to make a die

1. Take a cardboard tube.
2. Flatten the tube.
3. Cut the tube into two 4 cm pieces (the length may differ depending on the diameter of the tube).
4. Fold the tube in half again.
5. Now create a square face. Repeat with the second piece.
6. Push one inside the other and you should have a cube shape.

IDEA BANK

igh	ure	air	ear	sight words
night	sure	fair	fear	are
light	pure	hair	near	my
bright	cure	chair	tear	her
sight	mature	stair	clear	said
fight	secure	pair	dear	have
right	picture	repair	hear	like

1.
2.
3.
4.

Segmenting Structures

This activity focuses on Segmenting. Build some words but make sure to focus on the digraph sounds. Practise your segmenting by building some structures together.

What you need

Bricks (Duplo, Mega Bloks or Lego)

Dry erase marker

Preparation

Write letters onto bricks using a dry erase marker.

Activity

Say a word aloud.

Ask your child to count the sounds they can hear, and hold up that many fingers.

Your child then has to find the bricks they need, and build the word structure.

They will need to be careful, because some of the words in the idea bank have more than three sounds.

TOP TIP

As you approach Phase 4 phonics, the words will become more complex and some words will have four or more sounds.

Take your time to count the sounds you can hear in each of the words.

IDEA BANK

ai	ee	oa	oi	ar	or
brain	green	float	point	shark	north
train	street	throat	spoil	start	storm
chain	sleep	coach	joint	barn	short
trail	sweet	soap	boil	farm	born
paint	cheese	goat	join	yard	fork

ch a t
s t r e e t
b r ai n
g r ee n
sh

Paint Print Pictures

This activity focuses on Segmenting. Your child can make their own word book by printing and painting. This is a messy and creative activity.

What you need

Washable paints

Magnetic letters or paintbrush

Paper

Preparation

Fill a paint tray with some paint.

Activity

Let your child get messy and creative. Tell them to push the magnetic letters into the paint and use them to print onto the paper. Remind them to think about how the letter will print on the page. Let your child explore this and problem solve until the letters show up the correct way round.

What words can they create?

Allow the words to dry and stick the pages together to create a word book or poster.

TOP TIP

This activity could be created with any words or sounds you like. If your child needs a little extra support remembering all the Phase 3 digraphs, make a digraph book.

If you want to practise spelling sight words, give them a go.

The world is your child's oyster with this activity; encourage them to choose wisely and embrace the paint!

Playdough Dots and Dashes

This activity focuses on Blending. Use playdough to form dots for individual sounds and dashes for digraphs and trigraphs. Explore blending the sounds in words.

What you need

Word cards

Playdough

Two bowls

Preparation

Make your own word cards and cut them out (try using all the Phase 3 sounds).

Roll up small balls of playdough and place them in one bowl.

Make some small playdough dashes and place them in the second bowl.

Activity

Prompt your child to read the words on the cards and add the playdough dots and dashes underneath each of the words.

This is an activity that focuses on isolating each of the sounds to help your child spot the tricky sounds and decode complex words.

IDEA BANK

ch	sh	th UNVOICED	th VOICED	ng	ai	ee	igh	oa	oo LONG
cheese	shell	think	them	king	train	tree	high	goat	moon
chop	sheep	thin	those	song	main	bee	light	boat	food

ar	or	ur	ow	oi	ear	air	ure	er
star	fork	fur	cow	coin	ear	hair	pure	her
car	sort	burn	now	soil	near	chair	sure	term

shell

Become the Teacher

This activity focuses on Sound Recognition. Taking on the role of the teacher is a lot of fun, especially for children. Tell them you need help remembering all the sounds. Can they teach you?

What you need

Flashcards

Dry erase marker

Fancy dress costume (optional)

Preparation

When we play this game, we really commit! We get dressed up and become characters. We make it as fun as possible. You do not need to do this, but it will make you and your child enjoy it even more.

Activity

Sit cross-legged and prompt your child to 'become' the teacher. What can they teach you? Watch as your child shows you what they know.

They can use flashcards to practise the sounds. They could teach you some of the sight words or even help you to practise writing simple sentences.

Imaginary play is a fantastic tool for building confidence in your children.

TOP TIP

In this activity, take on the role of a child, make lots of mistakes and ask your children to help you.

Making mistakes is an essential part of learning and personal growth.

Show your child that it is good to make mistakes, and that mistakes are what help us to learn.

Facing and overcoming mistakes helps to build resilience. It teaches us to adapt and persist despite setbacks.

sleepy
sad
you
ee
What can
You see?

Story Sticks

This activity focuses on Letter Formation. Telling stories has never been so fun. Orally making up stories is just as beneficial as writing them, so give these story sticks a go; they are a fantastic tool for building our imaginations.

What you need

Three cups

Thirty craft sticks

Three coloured pens

Preparation

In a single colour, write ten character ideas on craft sticks.

In a second colour, write ten setting ideas on craft sticks.

In a third colour, write the names of ten objects on craft sticks. Place the sticks in separate cups.

Activity

Prompt your child to pull a stick from each cup.

Discuss the idea on each stick. Can your child describe their character, setting and object in more detail? What vocabulary can they come up with? What might happen in their story?

Tell each other your short stories. `

TOP TIP

Modelling some storytelling language and ideas is crucial in this activity.

Your child will be looking to you to help them to come up with some wonderful stories. Work together and see what you can create.

IDEA BANK

characters	settings	objects
bunny	forest	mirror
knight	beach	brush
owl	cave	map
mermaid	waterfall	compass
unicorn	castle	potion
pirate	mountain	keys
dragon	market	wand
frog	space	bag
fairy	shop	shoes
chicken	jungle	clock

AGE
5–6

Phase 4 phonics is typically taught to children during their second year of school, around the ages of five and six. This phase does not introduce any new sounds but focuses on consolidating knowledge from Phases 2 and 3 and developing fluency.

Phase 4 phonics is about building on the foundation laid in earlier phases, enhancing children's ability to decode and spell longer, more complex words.

By the end of Phase 4, children should be more confident readers and writers, ready to tackle the new challenges of Phase 5 phonics.

Scan QR code for an optional resource shortcut!

Phase 4 looks at five main aspects

Blending and Segmenting

In Phase 4, the focus is around reading and spelling fluently. In this phase children will be introduced to longer words and more complex spelling rules.

Adjacent Consonants

Children will learn lots of new adjacent consonants and understand that they can be found at the beginning, middle or end of words, for example **tr** in trip, **bl** in black and **nd** in hand.

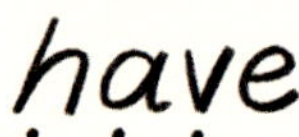

Sight Words

Children will be introduced to a list of new tricky words and continue to recall and practise the Phase 2 and Phase 3 sight words.

Polysyllabic Words

Using their knowledge of decoding, children will practise reading and spelling words with more than one syllable. For example, children, sandwich and handstand.

Sentences

Using all their knowledge, they will practise reading and writing longer and more complex sentences.

Blending and Segmenting

In this phase, children will be exposed to words that follow more complex patterns. In Phases 2 and 3, we predominantly looked at words that followed the CVC pattern. In Phase 4, children will be introduced to CCVC and CVCC words. For example, spot and tent.

Adjacent Consonants

Adjacent consonants are groups of two or three consonants that appear together in a word, with each consonant retaining its sound. They can appear at the beginning, middle or end of words.

Unlike digraphs (where two letters make one sound, like **sh** in ship), each adjacent consonant maintains its own sound. For example, in the word stop, the s and the t both make their own distinct sounds.

beginning	middle	end
bl (black, blue)	**nd** (windy, panda)	**mp** (lamp, jump)
cr (crab, crack)	**lp** (helping, alpaca)	**sk** (task, mask)
fl (flag, flip)	**nt** (winter, centre)	**nt** (went, plant)
gr (green, grow)	**lk** (walking, milkman)	
st (stop, star)		

Sight Words

In Phase 4 phonics, children are introduced to new sight words. These words often do not follow regular phonetic rules and need to be memorised by sight. Here is a list of the new sight words typically introduced in Phase 4: **said**, **have**, **like**, **so**, **do**, **some**, **come**, **were**, **there**, **little**, **one**, **when**, **out**, **what**

When introducing new sight words to your children, it is a good idea to use them in a sentence. Here are some sentence examples for each of the sight words:

said	Mummy said it was time for bed.
have	Do you have a pet?
like	I like to play with cars.
so	I am so happy to see you.
do	What do you want to do?
some	Can I have some pens please?
come	Will you come to my house?
were	They were playing in the park.
there	Look over there!
little	The little cat is very soft.
one	I have one sweet left.
when	When will we go home?
out	Let's go out and play.
what	What is your favourite colour?

Sight words can be tricky. There are lots of ways to practise at home:

Speed words: Try creating your own flashcards with one sight word on each card. Review them regularly to help your child recognise the words quickly.
Reading practice: Encourage your child to spot sight words while reading books. This helps reinforce recognition in different contexts.
Writing practice: Have your child practise writing the sight words. This helps with memorisation and reinforces their spelling.

Polysyllabic Words

A polysyllabic word is a word that contains more than one syllable. A syllable is a part of a word that contains a vowel sound. It is a single, unbroken sound in a word.

Understanding how to break down polysyllabic words into manageable syllables helps children read more fluently.

Here are some ways that you can explore polysyllabic words:

Clapping syllables: See the Clap & Stomp activity on page 46 for a fun way to explore syllables.
Visuals: Draw visual aids like syllable boxes in which each box represents a syllable in a word.
Chunking: Teach your child to look for smaller, familiar chunks or parts within a word to make it easier to read and spell. For example, in caterpillar, they might recognise cat and pill.

TOP TIPS

Try singing along to the Syllable Slide song that we discussed in Phase 3:

(Clap your hands)
All right now, we're gonna do the Syllable Slide!
Let's go to work!
To the left, two syllables.
(adult says the word ti-ger/ child claps twice)
Take it back, one syllable.
(adult says the word cat/ child claps once)

The full song can be found on page 282.

Sentences

Sentence writing in Phase 4 is designed to help children consolidate their phonics knowledge, develop their understanding of simple sentence structure and introduce some basic grammar rules.

The key aspects of sentence writing are:

Spelling: Children use phonics skills to spell words phonetically correctly.
Sight words: Using common words like 'the' and 'to'.
Sentence construction: Writing sentences that include nouns, verbs and adjectives.
Punctuation and grammar: Beginning to use capital letters at the start of sentences, full stops at the end and proper spacing between words.

In this chapter you will find sixteen activities covering all aspects of Phase 4 phonics. Take your time and enjoy each activity; they are designed to build confidence and spark some engagement during this consolidation phase.

Contents

TOP TIPS

As phonics becomes more complex it is even more important to make it fun and engaging for our children.

Continue to explore the sounds with actions.

Explore sentences but make them silly.

Remember, the more the children enjoy what they are learning, the more confidence and resilience they will build.

These activities can fit into your daily life without changing your routine. Let's encourage our children to enjoy learning!

Building Words

This activity focuses on Adjacent Consonants and Segmenting for spelling. How many words can your child build using the different word starters listed below?

What you need

Duplo or building blocks

Dry erase marker

Preparation

Write the adjacent consonants **sm**, **cl**, **st** and **fl** on five blocks each. You should have five blocks with **sm** written on them, five with **cl** and so on.

On the remaining blocks write a series of vowel digraphs, vowels and single consonants.

Activity

Prompt your child to focus on one adjacent consonant at a time. Say the sounds, practise how they sound together and then look at different words you can spell.

Say a word from the idea bank below and watch as your child finds the correct bricks. How many words can they make?

TOP TIP

Make sure you use a wide range of sounds. Remember all the sounds your child learned in Phase 3: **ch**, **sh**, **th**, **ng**, **ai**, **ee**, **oa**, **oo**, **oi**, **ar**, **or**, **ur**, **ow**, **er**, **igh**, **ear**, **air** and **ure**, as well as all the single sounds.

IDEA BANK

sm	cl	st	fl
smart	clean	stand	flash
smell	clip	start	float
smooth	cloud	stop	flock
smirk	clap	stick	floor
smash	clock	storm	flower

Note

Adjacent consonants are also known as clusters. They are two consonants that appear together that make two separate sounds.

cl
ou
d

Consonant Drops

This activity focuses on Adjacent Consonants and Blending for reading. Read the words and drop them into the correct tube.

What you need

Cardboard tubes

Tape

Paper

Pen

Preparation

Write the consonant clusters below onto cardboard tubes.

Tape the tubes to a wall.

Write the words from the idea bank below onto strips of paper.

Activity

Encourage your child to choose a slip of paper and read the word. What cluster is in the word? What two letters can they hear at the beginning of the word?

Tell your child to screw the slip of paper up into a ball and drop it into the correct tube.

How many words can they read? What cluster is the most challenging?

IDEA BANK

bl	cr	fr	gr	sl	pl	dr	tw	sw	sp
blue	crab	frog	green	slip	play	drag	twin	swim	spin
black	crash	fresh	grow	slow	plus	drop	twist	sweet	spot
blend	crop	from	grand	slug	plant	drip	twelve	swing	spell

Important information

Producing multiple consonant sounds in quick succession requires precise coordination of the tongue, lips and other speech skills. Young children are still developing these skills so they can be challenging for children still mastering basic phonemes.

Remember to take it slowly, isolate each of the sounds in the cluster and encourage your child to practise in a mirror.

spot
sw
cr
bl
fr
tw
dr
sl
sp
pl
gr
from
twelve
swing
crash
slip
spin
slug
blend
black
green
crop
slow
crab
spell
drop
plant
plus

Milky Way Words

This activity focuses on the recognition of Sight Words. Write out letters on a page that spell out sight words. Your child should then join them up to create their own constellations.

Preparation

Write the letters of a sight word on a small piece of paper, spaced out across the page. (Look at some simple constellations and try to mimic some of the shapes.)

What you need

Black paper

White pen/crayon

Activity

Say a sight word aloud and ask your child to draw a line connecting the letters in the correct order. If they manage to connect them correctly, you will be left with some night sky constellations. This is a basic game of dot to dot but instead it's letter to letter. Don't be alarmed if your pattern doesn't resemble a constellation at all. It is not essential.

TOP TIP

Sight word constellations are a teaching tool designed to help children recognise and remember sight words.

The idea of sight word constellations involves organising words in a visually engaging way, often resembling a constellation in the night sky, to make learning more interactive and fun.

IDEA BANK

said, have, like, so, do, some, come, were, there, little, one, when, out, what

t
h
e
r
e

Scavenger Hunt

This activity focuses on Segmenting and Polysyllabic Words. Scavenger hunts are a great way to get children moving, engaged and working on their phonics skills.

What you need

Paper

Pen

Preparation

Print/draw pictures or write a list of objects from around the house.

Activity

Give the list to your child and explain that today they are going on a scavenger hunt and they need to find all the objects you have listed. Can they read/write the words, find the objects and bring them to a designated space? Try to use a range of words to challenge your child.

TOP TIPS

Have a think about words that are polysyllabic and words that contain some trickier sounds.

How do you know if a word has more than one syllable? It has multiple vowels!

IDEA BANK

spoon, **pillow**, book, **toothbrush**, socks, chair, lamp, cup, pen, hat, **blanket**, scarf, **envelope**, **newspaper**, **crayon**, clock, **notebook**, **paper**, brush, **candle**, **lunchbox**, string, belt, plant

The words in **bold** are all polysyllabic words.

Digraph Family Dominoes

This activity focuses on decoding words with digraphs. Create some dominoes with coloured paper and play time and time again. This is a fun way to build confidence with blending skills.

Preparation

Make some domino cards using the digraphs listed below. Each side of the domino should have a word containing a different digraph.

What you need

- Paper
- Pens
- Scissors

Activity

Play a game of dominoes with your child, or encourage them to play with a sibling or other family member. This game focuses on spotting the digraph in a word, reading it aloud and then finding another word with the same digraph. This activity requires many skills, but lessens the cognitive load by isolating the trickier sounds first.

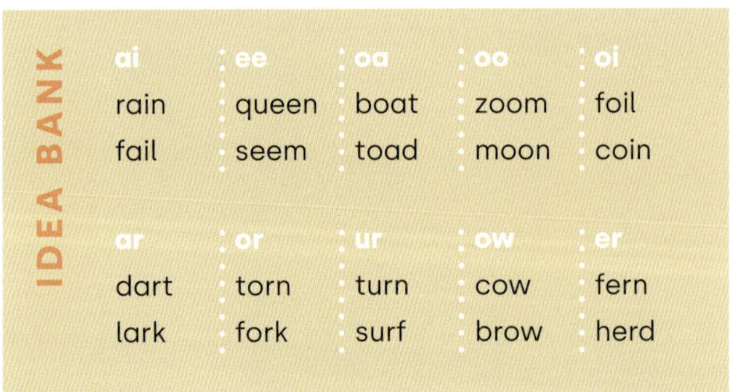

IDEA BANK

ai	ee	oa	oo	oi
rain	queen	boat	zoom	foil
fail	seem	toad	moon	coin

ar	or	ur	ow	er
dart	torn	turn	cow	fern
lark	fork	surf	brow	herd

food moon
zoom
seem torn
queen

Consonant Vowel Sort

This activity looks at the importance of understanding the different letters in the alphabet. Which letters are the most important and why? Can your children name the vowels and the consonants?

What you need

Magnetic letters

Two baskets

TOP TIPS 1

Recognising consonants and vowels helps children understand phonics and the relationship between letters and sounds.

Having knowledge of consonant and vowel patterns aids in spelling and helps children to learn common spelling rules and patterns, making it easier to spell words correctly.

TOP TIPS 2

Each of the vowels have a long and short sound.

The short sound is the sound that was taught in Phase 2 – c**a**t, b**e**d, f**i**g, d**o**g, b**u**n.

The long sound matches the way we say the vowel itself – m**a**ke, m**e**, h**i**, g**o** and h**u**ge.

Preparation

No preparation is needed for this activity.

Activity

Take a look at all the letters in the alphabet. Go through the letters one by one and discuss whether the letter is a vowel or a consonant. What can your child tell you about the vowels? Place the letters in the correct basket.

What do you think about the letter y? Discuss whether it is a vowel or a consonant.

When y is a vowel

At the end of words: my, try, fly, happy, funny.
When y appears at the end of a word and sounds like a long i or a long e, it acts as a vowel.

In the middle of words: gym, system, mystery, bicycle.
When y appears in the middle of a word and creates a vowel sound (often a short i), it functions as a vowel.

Fun Fact

The letter y can function both as a consonant and as a vowel in English, depending on its position and usage in a word.

Three in a Row

This activity focuses on Segmenting for spelling. Who will get three in a row first? Ask your child to listen to the word and recall what sounds they hear.

What you need

Pen

Paper

Pompoms

Preparation

Draw two noughts and crosses grids, with the sounds in different places on each of the grid.

Activity

Read a word from the idea bank below aloud.

Ask your child to segment the sounds in the words and recall the digraph or trigraph in the word. Then ask them to put a pompom on the digraph/trigraph that they heard in the word.

The first person to get three in a row is the winner!

IDEA BANK

oi	ear	ng	ch	oo	ure	ur	ow	sh
point	clear	strong	chair	bloom	manure	curl	brown	flash
foil	beard	bring	cheese	spoon	cure	burst	crown	brush
moist	rear	thing	lunch	food	endure	hurt	frown	shell

oi	ear	ng
ch	oo	ure
ur	ow	sh

sh
oo
ure
ng

Bin it!

This activity focuses on Blending for reading and looking at decoding unfamiliar words. Look very carefully at the words in the list because some of them are alien words!

Preparation

Write the list of words below on a piece of paper.

Cut them up so each word is on a separate piece of paper.

What you need

Paper

Pen

Scissors

A small bin

Activity

Encourage children to read the words on the pieces of paper. Can they spot the digraph sound first? Read the word aloud and ask them to decide whether they think this word is a real word or an alien word.

If it is a real word, put it in a nice, neat pile. If it is an alien word, screw it up and throw it in the bin!

TOP TIPS

In England at the end of Year One (typically children aged five to six), children sit a phonics screening test. In this test, children must decode forty words: twenty of the words are real words and twenty of them are pseudo words.

The purpose of the test is to assess a child's ability to decode words using their phonics knowledge, rather than relying on memorisation or context. This activity contains real words and alien words.

IDEA BANK

ai	oa	oi	or
snail	float	spoil	floor
kaid	doab	doik	dorb
trail	moag	coil	corn
chaib	goat	boif	hort
ee	**oo**	**ar**	**ur**
sleep	swoon	start	turn
freem	pooj	gark	gurj
creep	balloon	dart	surf
veen	lood	fard	durd

gark

CVCC Bowling

This activity focuses on Blending the sounds in words ending with Adjacent Consonants, for example tent. Create a game of bowling, explore blending the sounds and then knock them down.

What you need

Four or more cardboard tubes

Clear tape

Dry erase marker

Rubber or sponge

Ball

Preparation

Cover four cardboard tubes in clear tape.

Using a dry erase marker, write a letter on each of the cardboard tubes to spell out a word from the idea bank below.

Line the tubes up (if you use more than four tubes you can create a bowling triangle).

Activity

Place the cardboard tubes in a pile and ask your child to look at the sounds on the tubes. Can they put them in the right order to spell a word? See if they can unscramble the letters themselves. If this is too challenging, place the letters/sounds in a row to spell the four-letter word. Can they blend the letters together?

When they successfully read the word, they can have a go at knocking them down!

TOP TIP

CVCC words are often known as final consonant clusters – this is where you have a pair of consonants at the end of a word.

Common final consonant clusters are:

nd, st, ft, ld, mp, nk, nt

IDEA BANK

nd	ft	mp	nt
hand	gift	jump	tent
sand	lift	lamp	hunt
band	left	bump	plant
wind	swift	camp	grant
land	drift	stamp	point
pond	craft	cramp	front
grand	loft	dump	mint

st	ld	nk
list	cold	bank
fast	gold	tank
best	hold	pink
most	told	drink
nest	build	think
first	wild	link
last	field	blink

t e n t

Four-Letter Pull

This activity looks at Segmenting for Blending skills focusing on four-letter words, all containing a final consonant cluster.

What you need

Post-it notes

Pens

Preparation

Using the idea bank below, choose one of the word families and write each of the letters on a Post-it note, with one sound per Post-it.

Spell the first word out. Remember, consonant clusters are two sounds, not one. For example, nd is two sounds: **n** and **d**. So each of the words in this activity contain four sounds.

Activity

Using the Post-it notes, ask your child to create as many words as they can by changing one or more of the sounds. The final two letters should remain the same. For example, if you place an s on top of the h in hand it becomes sand.

Are all of the words real?

IDEA BANK

st	ft	ld	mp	nk	nd	nt
list	gift	cold	jump	bank	find	tent
bist	lift	gold	bump	tank	blind	hent
fist	left	hold	dump	thank	kind	hunt
quist	rift	told	lump	tink	mind	munt
chist	loft	fold	lamp	think	mend	mint
chest	poft	nold	gamp	blink	lend	wint

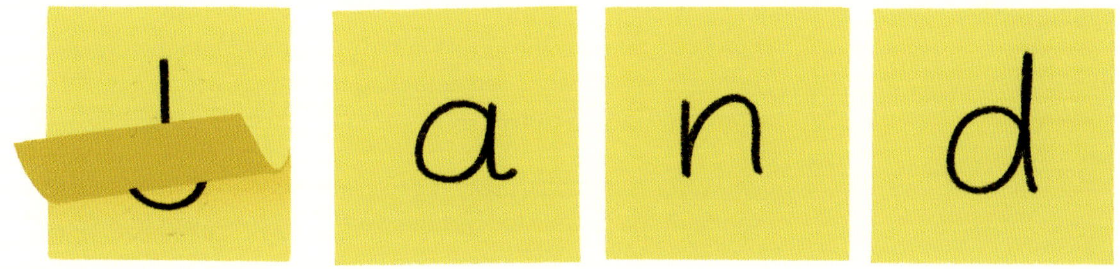
a
n
d

CCVCC Cups

This activity focuses on words that have Adjacent Consonants at their beginning and end. They can be particularly hard to sound out because they have five sounds in total. Give your child plenty of time!

What you need

Cups

Magnetic letters

Pen

Paper

Preparation

Spell some of the CCVCC words with magnetic letters and place them in the cups (one word per cup).

Draw a phoneme frame with five cells.

Activity

Let your child give one of the cups a shake, then take out the letters.

Ask them to place the letters in the correct order in the phoneme frame to spell a word, remembering that the vowel should always go in the middle.

What words can they create? Explore the different words, segment the sounds to spell the words and then read them back!

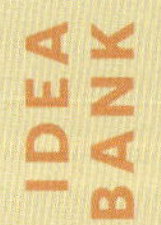

TOP TIPS

CCVCC words are words that begin with a consonant cluster, such as cl, and end with a consonant cluster, such as sp.

They always contain a single vowel sound in the middle.

IDEA BANK

brisk, crust, drank, frost, grant, plank, plant, print, smelt, stomp, trust, twist, trunk

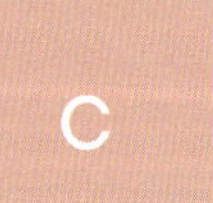

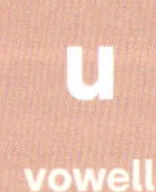
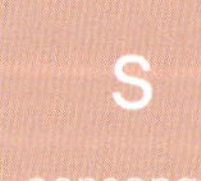

c	r	u	s	t
consonant	consonant	**vowell**	consonant	consonant

Playdough Eggs

This activity focuses on Sentences. Before children can begin writing their own sentences, they need to be able to read simple sentences. When they take a look inside the eggs, they may just find a sentence hiding.

What you need

- Playdough
- Paper
- Pen

Preparation

Write some short, simple sentences on a piece of paper.

Cut them up and fold them into small parcels.

Make some egg shapes from playdough and hide the sentences inside the eggs.

Place the eggs in a tray or basket and let your child find them.

Activity

Explain to your child that you have found this basket of eggs. Who do they think left them? What could be inside?

Open the eggs one by one and reveal the secret sentences written inside.

Support your child to read the simple sentences, decoding tricky words and remembering sight words.

TOP TIPS

You and your child can enjoy this activity in several different ways. Try to make it a fun sensory activity, but if you do not want to make playdough eggs, you could hide sentences in a sensory tray filled with sand, rice or dried chickpeas.

Allow your child to explore the sensory base and enjoy reading at the same time.

IDEA BANK

The frog jumps in the green pond.

Hand me the best gift please.

I can stand on the sand too.

The lamp is on the bedroom desk.

A pink dress is on the shop rack.

She will drink milk from the red cup.

The grand plant is next to the bench.

We must not jump on the bed.

The dog will hunt frogs in the field.

The crab grabs a rock.

lamp is on the

Syllable Sorting

This activity explores Polysyllabic Words and focuses on Blending for reading. It involves sorting words into cups. Always remember to sing the Syllable Slide (see page 282).

What you need

Three cups

Paper

Pen

Preparation

Write the numbers one, two and three on three cups.

Write the words from the idea bank below on slips of paper.

Activity

Read the words and ask your child to place them into the correct cup. Which words contain one syllable? Which contain two syllables?

If your child is finding it difficult, hand them the scissors and get them chopping the words into chunks – it always helps!

TOP TIP

If your child is finding polysyllabic words difficult to read, try cutting the words into syllable chunks. Prompt your child to read each chunk and blend them together. This lessens the cognitive load! For example, um-brel-la.

IDEA BANK

One syllable	Two syllables	Three syllables
jump	handstand	adventure
print	sunset	remember
blink	helmet	butterfly
twist	finger	calendar
drift	insect	happiness
crust	pumpkin	umbrella

1
2
3
twist
sunset
umbrella

Sentence Pictures

This activity focuses on Sentences. Forming and writing sentences can be tricky but often the trickiest part is thinking of what to write. Let's make some sentence pictures to help us to write some fun sentences.

What you need

Simple pictures of nouns

Paper

Pen

Glue stick

Preparation

Print and cut out a selection of clipart pictures from the idea bank below.

Activity

Take a look at the pictures and sort them into piles of people, animals, places and things.

Ask your child to choose some pictures from the piles and glue them together to make a funny picture sentence.

Prompt your child to write a sentence about each of their pictures.

Important information

A noun is a part of speech that refers to a person, place, thing or idea.

Today, we are looking at common nouns in four different categories: people, animals, places and things.

IDEA BANK

people	animals	places	things
mum	dog	beach	bench
dad	cat	shop	car
doctor	bunny	park	book
chef	chicken	home	pen

Sentence Expanders

This activity focuses on Sentence Writing. Expanding a sentence with adjectives and adverbs can make it more descriptive and engaging.

What you need

Craft sticks

Coloured pens

White board

Dry erase marker

Preparation

Write a series of adjectives on craft sticks in one colour and a series of adverbs in another colour.

Activity

Explain to your child what an adjective and an adverb are. Here is a simple way to explain what these are to your child: an adjective describes the noun, for example 'the dog is brown'; an adverb describes the way you do things, for example 'a baby cries loudly'.

They are going to use these special adjectives and adverbs to make their sentences more exciting. Prompt them to write one of the simple sentences below on their board.

Now they can choose an adjective stick and an adverb stick. Place the sticks in the correct place on their board and get them to read the sentence aloud. Talk about how it sounds a lot better now we know more!

Important information

Noun – person, place, thing or idea.

Verb – an action word.

Adjective – describes the noun.

Adverb – describes the verb.

IDEA BANK

Simple Sentences	Adjectives	Adverbs
The cat slept.	fluffy	soundly
The dog ran.	big	quickly
The bird sang.	colourful	sweetly
The boy smiled.	small	swiftly
The girl danced.	happy	loudly
The sun shone.	talented	gracefully
The car moved.	bright	slowly
The baby cried.	kind	clearly
The fish swam.		
The teacher spoke.		

gracefully
The big car moved quickly.
fluffy
happy
Small
talented
The girl

Tap it, Build it, Draw it, Write it!

This multi-sensory activity supports Segmenting for spelling while applying their knowledge of digraphs and trigraphs.

What you need

White board

Duplo, building blocks or magnetic letters

Dry erase marker

Preparation

Draw a grid on a white board with four boxes.

Write some letters on bricks (or just grab some magnetic letters).

Activity

In the first box draw dots and dashes – this will reflect how many sounds are in the word.

Say a word aloud for your child. Tell them to break the word up and tap it out using the first box on the grid.

Ask them to build the word with either magnetic letters or Duplo.

Then ask them to draw a simple picture of the word and, finally, to write it down.

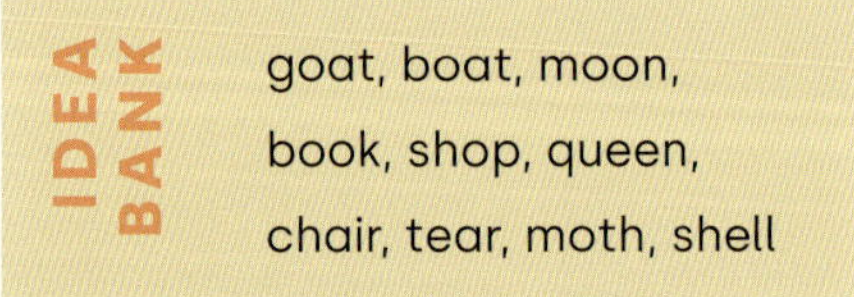
IDEA BANK

goat, boat, moon, book, shop, queen, chair, tear, moth, shell

build it
write it
draw it

AGE
5,6&7

Phase 5 phonics is typically taught to children during their second and third years of school, around the ages of five, six and seven. This phase covers new graphemes and begins to explore the more complex sound patterns and spelling alternatives found in the English language.

Phase 5 phonics focuses on learning different ways you can make the same sound.

We will begin to look at spelling rules and build upon all prior knowledge.

Phase 5 requires lots of practice and hands-on approaches!

Scan QR code for an optional resource shortcut!

Phase 5 looks at four main aspects

New Graphemes

Children encounter new graphemes, including **oe** (toe), **ew** (new), **au** (haul), **ou** (out), **ph** (phone), **wh** (when) and more.

Alternative Spellings

Children learn that sounds can be represented by different letters or combinations of letters. For example, the sound **ai** can be spelled as 'ai', 'ay', 'a-e' (split digraph) or 'eigh'.

Split Digraphs

Children learn about split digraphs, where a vowel sound is split by a consonant, such as **a-e** in make or **i-e** in time.

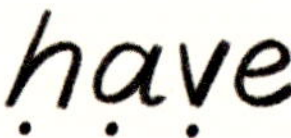

Sight Words

Children continue to learn and practise high-frequency words to build fluency in reading and writing.

New Graphemes

In Phase 5 phonics, children are introduced to several new graphemes. These new graphemes expand upon the knowledge gained in earlier phases and allow children to decode more complex words. This is truly when we begin to 'crack the code'.

Vowel Digraphs

ay – play
ou – out
ie – pie
ea – sea
oy – boy
ir – girl
ue – clue
aw – draw
wh – when

Tricky Digraphs

ph – dolphin
ew – new
oe – toe
au – launch

Other Graphemes

a (alternative sound) – was, watch
ey – money
e (alternative sound) – he, me

Alternative Spellings

Phase 5 also introduces children to alternative spellings for the sounds they already know. These alternative spellings introduce children to the idea that sounds can be represented by different letters or combinations of letters.

For example, the **ay** sound can be represented in lots of different ways. Let's look at the words snail, play, weigh and make. All of these letter combinations make the same sound.

a	**e**	**i**	**o**	**u**	**f**	**s**	**ch**	**er**	**oi**	**or**	**oo**	**ou**	**j**	**air**
ai	ee	igh	ow	u-e	ph	ss	tch	ir	oy	au	u-e	ow	g	are
ay	ea	i-e	oa		ff	c		ur		aw	ew			
a-e	e-e	y	o-e							al	ue			
eigh	ey	ie									ui			
aigh	y													
ey	ie													

Split Digraphs

Split digraphs are also sometimes known as 'magic e' or 'silent e'. They are called 'split' because the vowel sound is split by a consonant and ends with an 'e'. This 'e' is silent and doesn't make a sound, but it changes the pronunciation of the vowel name.

A rhyme that often helps children to remember is, 'Two vowels go walking but the first does the talking.'

a-e: cake, make, game, bake
e-e: theme, delete, trapeze, even
i-e: bike, kite, time, smile
o-e: bone, home, alone, phone
u-e: flute, brute/cube, compute

The **u-e** split digraph can make two different sounds: its vowel name, **u**, and the sound **oo**.

Sight Words

Here are the Phase 5 sight words to learn and practise: **Mr**, **Mrs**, **called**, **could**, **looked**, **don't**, **old**, **about**, **asked**, **I'm**, **house**, **your**, **very**, **by**, **time**, **came**, **make**, **their**, **day**, **saw**, **put**, **oh**, **people**, **here**

When introducing new sight words to your children it is a good idea to use them within a sentence. Here are some sentence examples for each of the sight words:

Mr: Mr Smith is our neighbour.
Mrs: Mrs Jones teaches at my school.
called: She called her friend on the phone.
could: I could swim when I was younger.
looked: The cat looked at the bird in the tree.
don't: Don't forget to brush your teeth before bed.
old: My grandma has an old car.
about: Let's talk about your favourite book.
asked: She asked her mum for help with homework.
I'm: I'm going to the park with my friends.
house: We have a yellow house with a red door.
your: Is that your pencil on the desk?
very: The cake was very delicious.
by: We walked by the river on our hike.
time: It's time to go to bed.
came: The postman came to deliver a package.

TOP TIPS

When introducing split digraphs, I tell children that the two letters are best friends but when they are together they talk too much, so their teacher always makes another letter sit between them. This changes the way they sound for everyone else and makes the 'e' silent

make: Let's make a picture for Grandma.
their: The children brought their toys to the park.
day: It is a sunny day.
saw: I saw a rainbow after the rain.
put: Put your shoes on before going outside.
oh: Oh, look at the pretty flowers!
people: There are many people at the park today.
here: Come here and sit next to me.

Sentences

In Phase 5 of phonics, children focus on reading and writing sentences that include the graphemes and phonemes they have learned so far.

Reading/decoding practice: Children read sentences containing Phase 5 graphemes, digraphs, trigraphs and split digraphs. These sentences often include a mix of real and alien words and sight words.

Sentence building: Children learn to construct sentences using Phase 5 graphemes and sight words. They learn about basic grammar rules and punctuation, such as capital letters, punctuation marks such as full stops and question marks and basic sentence structure.

In this chapter you will find sixteen activities that cover all elements of the Phase 5 curriculum. They are designed to build confidence and spark joy.

Contents

FUN SPELLING RULES FOR PHASE 5

'Magic e': When a word has a silent e at the end, for example, 'cake' and 'bike'.

Double up: When a one-syllable word ends in an **f**, **l**, **s** or **z** sound, double up: for example, huff, hill, kiss and buzz.

Soft c and g: Sometimes, c and g can be soft and make their **s** and **j** sounds. When c is followed by e, i or y, it says **s** like in 'ice'. When g is followed by e, i or y, it says **j** like in 'giraffe'. Soft as a whisper!

Bossy vowels: When you see two vowels together in a word, like ai or oa, the first one usually says its name, and the second one is silent. For example, 'boat' and 'rain'. The first vowel is the bossy vowel!

Pronunciations

This activity focuses on Alternative Sounds. Did you know that vowels have a long sound and a short sound? This activity looks at words using the different vowel sounds!

What you need

- White board
- Pen
- Paper
- Scissors
- Highlighter

Preparation

Write the words from the idea bank below on paper and cut them up.

Draw the grid opposite on a white board.

Activity

Invite your child to take a look at each of the words and use a highlighter to highlight the vowels in the word.

Get them to try reading one word at a time to work out if it has a long or short sound, then put it in the correct column. (Remembering that sometimes y is a vowel!)

Explore each of the words and look at the rules.

Short vowel sounds are often created if there is one vowel (a, e, i, o, u) in a single syllable word. For instance, bug, pen and long. If a vowel is followed by a single consonant at the end of a word, or by two different consonants, it is usually short. For example, cat, pin and kick.

TOP TIP
Vowels change their sound based on where they are located in a word and what letters are around them.

IDEA BANK

long a	long e	long i	long o	long u
acorn, cake, paint, train, make, apron, car, far	eve, complete, team, meat, be, me, her, term	bike, kite, pie, tie, hi, fly, bird, girl	bone, home, boat, road, o, no, horn, born	use, tune, true, suit, human, unit, turn, burn

short a	short e	short i	short o	short u
cat, hat, bat, map, bag	bed, red, pen, met, leg	sit, hit, bit, lid, fig	hot, pot, box, dog, log	cup, sun, run, hug, bus

Long vowel sounds are often created when two vowels appear side by side in a syllable. When vowels work as a team to make a long vowel sound, the second vowel is silent. Such as, goat, sleep and rain.

A vowel at the end of a syllable is almost always long. For example, he, we, be, tomato.

An r-controlled vowel is when an r appears after the vowel, changing the way it sounds. It doesn't make its typical long sound. For instance, car, her.

long	short
acorn	cat
be	bed

Split Prints

This activity focuses on New Graphemes. Learning about split digraphs can be tricky but this activity provides some fun tricks to help us!

What you need

- Playdough
- Magnetic letters
- Child-safe knife

Preparation

No preparation is needed for this activity.

Activity

Let your child explore making prints in playdough using magnetic letters. Ask them how they can spell words with split digraphs? What letter must come at the end?

Remember these words are all using their long vowel sound so practise the vowel song on page 283.

✓ TOP TIPS

A split digraph is a two-letter grapheme where the letters are split by a consonant, resulting in a long vowel sound.

Here are few simple ways you can remember this:

1 Two vowels go walking but the first does the talking.

2 Two vowels are best friends but they talk too much, so a consonant must sit in between them. When the vowels are split up, only the first sound talks and it always says its name!

3 These words always end with a bossy e. The bossy e comes along to all the parties even when he isn't invited!

IDEA BANK

a-e	e-e	i-e	o-e	u-e
cake	these	bike	bone	cube
make	theme	kite	home	use
name	scene	time	rope	tune
gate	eve	line	note	mule
plane	delete	shine	stone	fume

Sentence Subs

This activity focuses on Sentence Reading and Writing. Make up some sentences together. Watch as you change one word in the sentence and how it can change everything!

What you need

White board

Dry erase markers (two different colours)

TOP TIP 1

Nouns – A noun is a part of a sentence that refers to a person, place or thing.

Verbs – A verb is an action word that refers to the action that the person is doing.

TOP TIP 2

To prolong this activity, you can also change the verb.

For example:

The cat sat on the grass.

The cat jumped on the chicken.

Here we have changed the noun and the verb.

Preparation

Write the sentence 'The **cat** sat on a **mat**' on the white board. The nouns are highlighted here; you could use a different colour pen to make them stand out.

Activity

Give your child the white board and ask them to read the sentence.

Discuss what a noun is.

Prompt your child to change the nouns in the sentence to make funny sentences. For example: The cat sat on my head.

You can do this multiple times to make lots of different sentences. Practise reading and writing sentences together.

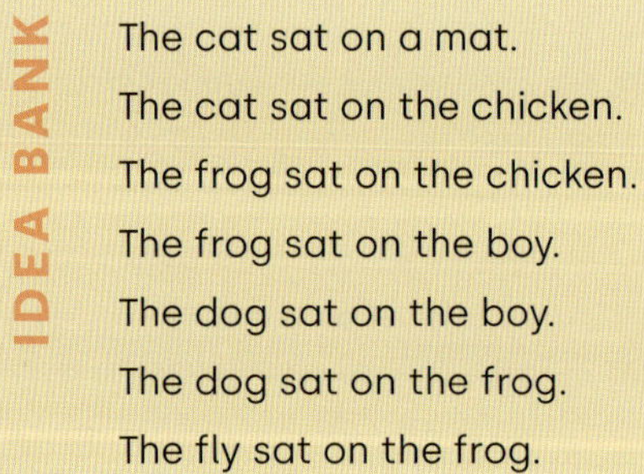

'Magic e'

This activity focuses on New Graphemes. Sometimes you just need a magic wand to help you to spell!

Preparation

Write the nonsense words from the idea bank below onto paper and cut them out.

Grab some crafty materials to make your child's wand magnificent.

What you need

Paper

Pens

Craft stick

Craft materials – glitter, string, ribbons, sequins

Activity

Help your child to make a 'magic e' wand. Use a craft stick or wooden dowel to make a wand. Wrap it in string, paint it, add glitter – make it wonderful. Place an 'e' on the end of the wand.

Prompt your child to add the 'magic e' to the end of the printed nonsense words and explore how it changes.

Discuss what happens. Some of the words will go from nonsense words to REAL words – they change from the short vowel sound to the long vowel sound.

TOP TIPS

See page 198 for all previous tricks and rules surrounding the Split Digraphs.

Remember to sing the vowel song to practise saying the vowel names!

IDEA BANK

a	e	i	o	u
mak	pet	smil	phon	hug
shak	complet	shin	bon	brut
nam	trapez	bik	hom	cut
gat	delet	kit	con	cub

brut
con
shin
hug
shak
delet
kit
gat
e
bik
nam
trapez
bon

Sight Word Ping-Pong

This activity focuses on Sight Words. A fun game of ping-pong, helping us to practise reading tricky sight words.

What you need

Cups

Paper

Scissors

Ball

Preparation

Write the words from the idea bank below onto paper and cut into small slips. Fold the slips and place them into cups.

Arrange the cups on a table in a triangle shape.

Activity

Take turns with family members to throw or bounce a ball into the cups.

If you land a ball, remove it and read the word inside the cup.

Ask your child which words they find difficult. Is there a way that they can remember some of the tricky words? Some of these words have a split digraph – which ones?

IDEA BANK

Mr, Mrs, called, could, looked, don't, old, about, asked, I'm, house, your, very, by, time, came, make, their, day, saw, put, oh, people, here

TOP TIP

Most sight words follow different rules. Take a look at each of the words with your child and work out which sounds are trying to trick us!

ut
hou

Roll and Write

This activity focuses on Sight Words. Each face of the dice corresponds to a sight word. When you roll that number on the die you must write the word.

What you need

Dice

White board

Dry erase marker

Preparation

Make a key with the numbers and the words.

Activity

Explain the rules of the game. Tell your child to roll the dice and write the word. Say the word aloud and ask your child to write it down. It is as simple as that!

Ask them if they can use the word within a spoken sentence. Can they write out the whole sentence?

TOP TIPS

Mnemonics can help when learning different sight words.

Here are some fun mnemonics to help with these sight words:

Called – **C**an **a**ll **l**ittle **l**ions **e**at **d**inner?

Could – **C**ats **o**nly **u**se **l**itter **d**aily

Looked – **L**ions **o**ften **o**verlook **k**ind **e**lephants **d**ancing

Old – **O**nly **l**ittle **d**ogs

About – **A** **b**ear **o**ften **u**ses **t**ools

Red die	Blue die
1 – called	1 – asked
2 – could	2 – I'm
3 – looked	3 – house
4 – don't	4 – your
5 – old	5 – by
6 – about	6 – their

Red Die	Blue Die
1. called	1. asked
2. could	2. I'm
3. looked	3. house
4. don't	4. your
5. old	5. by
6. about	6. their

So Many Ways

This activity focuses on Alternative Sounds. Did you know that you can make the a sound in lots of different ways? Let's explore seven different grapheme sets! Write words on craft sticks and get your child to put the sticks in the right cup.

What you need

Cups

Craft sticks (optional)

Preparation

Write the seven different ways of making the a sound on cups. There are three common ways – **ai**, **ay**, **a-e** – and four rare ways – **ea**, **aigh**, **eigh**, **ey**.

Write the words from the idea bank below on craft sticks or on slips of paper.

Activity

Encourage your child to read the words and place them in the cup that corresponds with the way that word makes the a sound.

IDEA BANK

ai	ay	a-e	ea
rain	day	cake	steak
train	play	make	break
brain	stay	name	great
paint	tray	plate	
mail	may	skate	
Usually found in the middle.	*Usually found at the end.*	*Always has a consonant in the middle and found at the end.*	*Usually found in the middle.*

aigh	eigh	ey
straight	eight	they
	weight	grey
	sleigh	obey
Could this be the only one?	*Usually found in the middle.*	*Usually found at the end.*

✓

TOP TIP

When learning alternative spellings, it is important to teach children that while there are often rules we can learn to help us to remember, there are also lots of exceptions. That is why it is important to practise.

Simple rules: Teach simple rules first, such as **ai** usually comes in the middle of a word (r**ai**n), and **ay** usually comes at the end of a word (pl**ay**).

Exceptions: Gently introduce the idea that English has exceptions and that it's OK to make mistakes while learning; mistakes help us to learn.

You will find some 'rules' in the idea bank opposite.

ai
ay
a-e
ea
aigh
eigh
ey
grey
great
tray
make
eight
straight
paint
cake
break
steak
sleigh

Two or Three

This activity focuses on New Graphemes. Find them, recognise them and sort them. Sort the digraphs from the trigraphs and the split digraphs.

Preparation

Write the words from the idea bank below onto slips of paper.

Make a three-column grid and label the columns with digraph, trigraph and split digraph.

What you need

Paper

Pens

Highlighter

Activity

Ask your child to choose a word from the pile and highlight the 'best friend' sound they can see in the word. What do they know about that sound?

Ask them to place the word into the correct column.

Can they think of a special rule for each of the new sounds? Where does it sit in the word, the beginning, middle or end? What have they learned about this list of words?

TOP TIPS

This is an activity that helps children to understand the different sounds you find in words.

By looking at the sound first, your child will find it easier to read the word as it lessens the cognitive load.

Remember to refer to these graphemes as best friends. They work together to make a new sound!

IDEA BANK

ay	ou	ie	ea	oy	ir	ue
play	shout	pie	team	joy	whirl	blue
aw	wh	ph	ew	oe	au	
yawn	whale	phone	screw	toe	haul	
igh	ure		air	ear		
night	manure		fair	spear		
a-e	e-e		i-e	o-e	u-e	
cake	complete		smile	home	huge	

digraph	trigraph	split digraph
joy	spear	home
play		

Sound Snipping Syllables

This activity focuses on New Graphemes. How many syllables are in the words? What do you notice about each of the syllables?

What you need

Paper

Pencils

Scissors

Preparation

Write the words in large print on slips of paper.

Activity

Provide your child with the polysyllabic words and a pair of scissors. Explain that it is their job to decode the word and then chunk the word into its syllables. For example, en-coun-ter.

Next, look at each of the syllables in the word and encourage your child to think about what sounds they can see and whether each of the sounds are a vowel or consonant.

Each syllable contains at least one vowel!

TOP TIPS

Remember that every syllable has at least one vowel, so look out for the vowels to help you with chunking.

If your child is finding it difficult to decipher how many syllables are in the word, practise saying the word aloud together and count the syllables as your child repeats the word.

IDEA BANK

two-syllable	three-syllable	four-syllable	five-syllable
daylight	creation	enjoyable	irresistible
playground	encounter	irrational	abracadabra
mountain	royalty	transportation	electricity
annoy	miracle	information	communication
awkward	influence	helicopter	creativity
sawdust	avenue	technology	appreciation

en coun ter

Lie Detector

This activity focuses on Polysyllabic Words. In this game your child is the lie detector and must find out the truth. Which sounds are lying and what words just want us to know the truth?

What you need

Paper

Pencil

Envelopes

Stopwatch or timer

Preparation

Write the statements below onto pieces of paper and place them into envelopes.

Hide the envelopes around the house.

Activity

Explain to your child that today, they have become the LIE DETECTOR! It is their job to find all the hidden envelopes around the house. Set a timer and let them start hunting. When they find an envelope, they must read the statement inside and decide whether the statement is true or false. Will they find all the envelopes in the time limit?

STATEMENT BANK

1 The word **summer** has two syllables and four sounds. (True)
2 The word **forest** has two vowels. (True)
3 The word **happiness** has three syllables and only one double letter digraph. (False)
4 The word **computer** has four syllables. (False)
5 The word **invisible** contains four i's and four syllables. (False)
6 **Necessary** is spelled correctly and has four syllables. (True)
7 **Celebration** has a soft c at the beginning and has three syllables. (False)
8 The word **independent** has five syllables. (False)
9 The word **communication** has three syllables. (False)
10 **Elephant** has three syllables. (True)

Misunderstood

Rule Breakers

This activity focuses on Alternative Spellings. Some digraphs do not follow simple rules so it is hard to know when to use the correct one. Practise makes perfect, so let's practise!

What you need

- Two baskets
- Paper
- Pencils
- Highlighter

Preparation

Write all the words from the idea bank below onto paper and cut them into slips – one word per slip.

Place the words into piles of the same sound, for example words with ee and ea sounds go in the same pile.

Activity

Prompt your child to look at all the words in front of them, read the word and highlight the digraph in the word. Notice how the sounds are the same but they are spelled differently. Are there any rules that differentiate the two sounds?

IDEA BANK

ai/ay	ee/ea	igh/ie	ow/oa	er/ur	oi/oy	or/aw	oo/ew	ou/ow
rain	sleep	night	goat	letter	coil	torn	poo	shout
pain	cheep	flight	boat	better	boil	corn	zoo	out
chain	keep	knight	float	fern	foil	thorn	moon	about
play	team	tie	blow	turn	boy	yawn	screw	brown
stay	steam	pie	snow	churn	toy	dawn	shrew	cow
away	stream	lie	crow	burn	joy	draw	blew	frown

TOP TIPS

For this activity it is important to only practise one sound at a time with two alternative spellings. This way children can focus on practising slowly and thoroughly.

ou
shout
blow
about
float
boat
oa
goat
cow
crow
ow
ow

Compound Words

This activity focuses on Polysyllabic Words and Complex Sounds. Some two- and three-syllable words are compound words, but what is a compound word? Let's find out!

What you need

Post-it notes

Pens

Preparation

Write each of the compound words on Post-it notes with one syllable on each Post-it. For example, football = foot and ball.

Muddle up all the words and leave them on a flat surface.

Activity

Explain to your child that a compound word is a two-syllable word made up of two simple words.

Prompt your child to find a matching pair of two words that come together to make a new compound word. Some of these three syllable words are not compound words. Can your child work out which ones?

TOP TIPS

A compound word is typically a two-syllable word that is made up of two words, for example lunchbox. They make sense on their own and together.

IDEA BANK

two-syllable	three-syllable
football	sunflower
rainbow	butterfly
notebook	firefighter
hairbrush	grandmother
toothpaste	sunglasses
snowman	jellyfish
birdhouse	confetti
cupcake	direction
homework	cucumber
playground	beautiful
blackboard	difficult
bedroom	fantastic

man
cup
bow
note
foot
ball

Homographs vs Homophones

This activity is split into two separate tasks and focuses on New Graphemes and Complex Sounds. Homographs and homophones are tricky! Let's find out what they are.

What you need

Paper

Pencil

Dinner plate

Basket

Note
You can complete this activity in two sessions if you would like to focus on homographs in one session and homophones in the other.

TOP TIPS
A homograph is a word that is spelled the same as another word but has a different meaning and sometimes a different pronunciation.

A homophone is a word that is pronounced the same as another word but has a different meaning, and often a different spelling.

HOMOGRAPHS

Preparation

Draw a circle on the paper using a dinner plate as a template.

Divide the circle into segments like pizza slices.

Write a homograph on each segment.

Activity 1 – Homographs

Ask your child to place a pencil in the middle of the circle, spin it and wait until it lands on one of the words. Discuss the word that it landed on. What does it mean? Can they think of both meanings?

HOMOPHONES

Preparation

Draw a circle on the paper using a dinner plate as a template.

Divide the circle into segments like pizza slices.

Write a homophone on each segment.

On slips of paper write the matching homophones to those written on the segments. For example, write bear on a segment of the circle and also write bear on a slip of paper.

Activity 2 – Homophones

Spin the pencil and find the matching homophone for whatever it lands on.

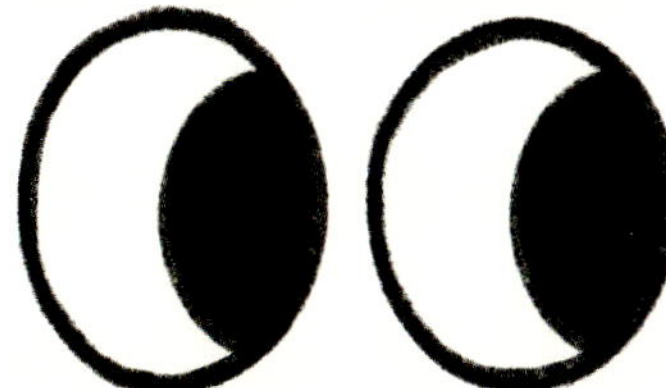

IDEA BANK

homographs	Homophones
bow (in hair), bow (to royalty)	to, too, two
wind (outside), wind (up the Jack-in-the-box)	their, there, they're
scale (weighing scale), scale (on a fish)	bear, bare
spring (season), spring (in a chair)	piece, peace
mouse (animal), mouse (computer)	night, knight
bark (dog), bark (on a tree)	here, hear
nail (on your hand), nail (and hammer)	tale, tail
change (money), change (your clothes)	blue, blew

Sound Book

This activity focuses on New Graphemes. Over the course of a week, your child can make a sound book with all the different digraphs and trigraphs they know.

What you need

Paper

Paint or felt-tip pens

Preparation

Compile some craft materials and you are ready to get started!

Activity

Ask your child whether they would like to make their own book, poster or flashcards and prompt them to write out a list of all the sounds they can remember.

Say some words aloud for them to recall the sounds and write them down.

Now they are ready to design their own. They should make them as exciting and beautiful as possible.

While you are making and creating, talk about each of the sounds. What letters do they have in them? How many vowels? What words can they think of containing that sound?

This is a brilliant opportunity to talk about phonics in an informal way. You may even find out little snippets of information about their learning at school.

Crafting is like therapy for lots of children. Arts and crafts provide a creative and supportive outlet for children to express and explore their emotions. It fosters communication, self-expression and emotional understanding, which are essential for their emotional development and wellbeing.

TOP TIPS

This activity aims to look at all the new sounds from Phase 5. What sounds can your child recall and what do they know about each of the sounds? This is a great opportunity to discuss any sounds that your child may have found difficult. You can make this into a book, flashcards or poster.

Dig it Up!

This activity focuses on Reading and Writing Sentences. Reading and writing sentences can be difficult, so here's an activity to make it fun. Let's go digging.

Preparation

Fill a tray with sand.

Cut out some bone shapes from the paper, and write some sentence-starters on them.

Hide them in the sand.

What you need

A tray

Sand

Paper

Scissors

Pen

Activity

Let your child dig in the sand to find a bone. When they uncover one, ask them to read the sentence-starter and finish the sentence or story.

Encourage them to use their imagination to come up with some amazing stories.

For a bonus challenge, ask them to write their story down.

These sentence-starters can spark imaginative stories, personal reflections or creative descriptions, encouraging children to express themselves through spoken or written language. They provide a fun and engaging way to prompt storytelling and communication skills.

TOP TIPS

Sensory activities make learning phonics more engaging and interesting for children. By incorporating tactile, auditory and visual sensations, it captures a child's attention and encourages active participation in learning.

IDEA BANK

One sunny day ...

In a faraway land ...

My favourite thing to do is ...

I like to imagine ...

Today, I discovered ...

If I could have any superpower, I would ...

My pet (or imaginary friend) and I ...

In my dream last night ...

At the park, I found ...

Explode a Sentence

This activity focuses on Sentence Structure and Writing. This is a game and the winner is the person with the most points. You win points for words added to your simple sentence.

What you need

White board

Dry erase marker

Die

Preparation

Write one of the simple three-word sentences from the idea bank below on the white board.

Activity

Start with a simple three-word sentence that follows this formulation: The (noun) (verb).

Each person takes turns rolling the die. You must add that number of words to your sentence to win a point for each word. You can add adjectives, adverbs and prepositional phrases. Your sentence must make sense.

IDEA BANK

The tree grows.
The flower blooms.
The river flows.
The bird chirps.
The fish swims.
The bear sleeps.
The clock ticks.
The wind blows.
The baby crawls.
The rabbit hops.

Example

The tree grows.
roll a one

The tall tree grows.
roll a one

The tall oak tree grows.
roll a one

The tall oak tree grows slowly.
roll a three

In the forest, the tall oak tree grows slowly.
roll a four

In the lush green forest, the tall oak tree grows gracefully and slowly.
roll a five

Underneath the bright morning sun, in the lush green forest, the tall oak tree grows gracefully and slowly.

Noun
A noun is a word used to name a person, place, thing.

Verb
A verb is a word that expresses an action

Adjective
An adjective is a word that describes a noun

Adverb
An adverb is a word that describes a verb

Prepositional phrase
A prepositional phrase is a group of words that begins with a preposition and usually ends with a noun, for example 'under the table' or 'in the house'.

clock ticks.
clock ticks slowly.
In the hauted
the clock ticks
the
DRY ERASE

AGE
6–7

Phase 6 phonics is typically taught to children during their third year of school, around the ages six to seven. This phase covers new concepts like suffixes and word endings, plurals, prefixes and understanding the past tense. Phase 6 is the final stepping stone in phonics which aims to prepare children for fluent reading and writing.

Phase 6 phonics is the stage at which children start to become fluent readers and accurate spellers.

They will have learned most of the graphemes and phonemes in the English language and will be able to read and spell words without sounding them out.

Scan QR code for an optional resource shortcut!

Phase 6 looks at five main aspects

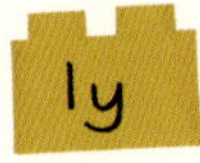

Suffixes and prefixes

Children learn about suffixes, such as -s, -es, -ing, -ed and how they change the meaning of a word. They also explore prefixes, for example un-, re-, dis- and how they change the meaning of root words.

Plurals and spelling patterns

Children learn about plurals by adding -s or -es to the end of words. They begin to explore irregular plurals, such as mice, children.

Children learn about different spelling patterns and rules and apply this knowledge in their reading and writing. For example, to make the past tense of a word that ends in a single vowel and consonant you must double the final consonant before adding -ed. Hop becomes hopped.

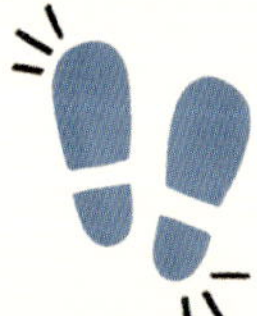

Past tense

Children explore and consolidate their learning around past-tense vocabulary and are introduced to the concept of regular (walked) and irregular (went) past-tense verbs.

Dictionary use

Children begin to understand how and when to use a dictionary to support their reading, writing and understanding.

Reading and writing fluency

Phase 6 focuses on developing fluency in reading and writing by applying phonics skills with increasing speed and accuracy.

Suffixes and prefixes

A suffix is a letter or a group of letters attached to the **end** of a word to form a new word or change the grammatical function of the word. Children learn about the most common suffixes for example, -s, -es, -ing, -ed, -able, -ly.

They also explore how adding these suffixes affects the spelling and pronunciation of base words, for example adding -ing to jump makes jumping.

A prefix is a letter or a group of letters attached to the **beginning** of a word that partly indicates its meaning.

For example, the word prefix itself begins with the prefix pre-, which means before or in front of. Children explore the most common prefixes for example, un-, re-, dis- and how they change the meaning of root words.

They also learn to identify and use common prefixes correctly in their writing.

Plurals

A plural noun means more than one. By adding -s to the end of nouns, it changes a singular to a group. In Phase 6, children learn to identify regular plural nouns and irregular plural nouns. They will also begin to learn simple rules to help them with their spelling:

Just add -s
apple – apples
cat – cats
tree – trees

If it ends in s, ch, sh, zz or x, add -es
bus – buses
fox – foxes
lunch – lunches

If it ends in y, drop the y and add -ies
baby – babies
story – stories
lady – ladies

If it ends in f or fe, drop the f or fe and add -ves
leaf – leaves
life – lives
shelf – shelves

Irregular plural nouns are those that do not follow any spelling rules and the word often changes entirely when it becomes a plural. For example, foot becomes feet, man becomes men, child becomes children, tooth becomes teeth.

Past Tense

Teaching children about the past tense in Phase 6 phonics involves a focus on spelling rules, suffixes, and regular and irregular verbs.

Regular verbs

These follow a consistent pattern when forming the past tense by adding -ed. For example, walked and played. A lot of this would have been covered while looking at suffixes.

Irregular verbs

These do not follow the regular pattern and have unique past tense forms, such as went, ate and saw.

Dictionary use

Children will learn to use a dictionary to support their writing and vocabulary development. They will look at:

Alphabetical order

Children learn that dictionaries list words in alphabetical order. They practise locating words based on their initial letters.

Word definitions

Children are taught to look up unfamiliar words to find their meanings.

Spelling and word forms
Children practise checking spellings and finding different forms of words, such as plurals and past-tense forms, in the dictionary.

Usage examples
Children learn that dictionaries often provide examples of how words are used in sentences.

Reading and writing fluency

Phase 6 focuses on developing fluency in reading and writing by applying phonics skills with increasing speed and accuracy. Children practise reading and writing sentences, stories and non-fiction texts that incorporate the phonics principles they have learned throughout all six phases.

This phase sees the end of the phonics curriculum, but it certainly does not need to be the end of phonics. Phonics is something that you can always lean back on to support decoding and complex spellings.

In this chapter you will find sixteen activities that cover all elements of the Phase 6 curriculum. They are designed to develop fluency and accuracy in reading and spelling.

This chapter has been designed to be enjoyed by children aged six to seven. After completing Phase 6, your child's phonics journey is complete, but that does not mean your journey should end. Phonics should remain an enjoyable way of remembering spelling rules and patterns beyond the age of seven!

Contents

FUN SPELLING RULES FOR PHASE 6

1 Adding -ed and -ing to verbs
Rule: Add -ed for past tense and -ing for present continuous tense.

2 Doubling consonants
Rule: Double the final consonant before adding -ed or -ing if the verb ends in a vowel consonant pattern, for example hop becomes hopped and hopping.

3 Changing -y to -i-
Rule: Change -y to -i before adding -ed or other suffixes if the word ends in a consonant followed by -y, for example carry becomes carried.

4 Adding -es to words ending in -s, -ss, -sh, -ch, -x, or -z
Rule: Add -es to form the plural of words ending in -s, -ss, -sh, -ch, -x, or -z, for example box becomes boxes.

5 Dropping the silent 'e'
Rule: Take off the e and add -ing, for example hope becomes hoping.

Verb Charades

This activity focuses on Past and Present Tense. Fill a cup with different verbs (past and present tense). Try acting them out for someone to guess.

What you need

- Paper
- Pencils
- Cup

Preparation

Write the verbs from the idea bank below onto slips of paper.

Fold each of the pieces of paper up and place into a cup.

Activity

Take it in turns to pull out a verb, read it and act it out for your opponent to guess.

This activity supports reading and understanding different vowel tenses and explores the use of -ed at the end of words.

For an added challenge, ask your child to try writing each of the words after the game has ended.

TOP TIPS

The words in the idea bank are all regular verbs: their past-tense form can be made by adding -ed to the end.

Explore reading each of the words and looking at the spelling.

Try giving your child a coloured pen and speaking about how the word has been changed into a different tense – can they highlight the word ending?

IDEA BANK

present tense	past tense
bake	cleaned
call	danced
jump	looked
listen	opened
play	pushed
smile	talked
walk	watched

Past Tense Time

This activity focuses on Past and Present Tense. This is a game of matching pairs like no other; it focuses on words with the same meaning but in two different tenses.

What you need

Paper

Pencil or pens

Preparation

Write each of the twenty-four verbs from the idea bank below onto playing-card-sized pieces of paper.

Lay out the cards, face down, in a grid.

Activity

This is just like a game of matching pairs, but as well as being a game of matching it's also a game of memory. Ask your child to turn two cards over at a time and read the words that are revealed. Do they have the same meaning but in a different tense? For example, catch and caught. If the answer is yes, they are a matching pair. Enjoy exploring the meaning of each of the words and look at the spellings of each of the words.

TOP TIPS

This activity looks at regular and irregular verbs.

You can change lots of present-tense verbs into past-tense verbs just by adding -ed; these are called regular verbs.

However, there are lots of verbs that do not follow the pattern and change altogether for their past-tense form, making them irregular verbs.

Let's explore these words together!

IDEA BANK

present tense	past tense
begin	began
break	broke
bring	brought
catch	caught
eat	ate
fly	flew
leave	left
make	made
meet	met
say	said
sing	sang
take	took

said
bring
made
brought
leave
say
caught
catch
left

Three Ways

This activity focuses on Spelling Rules. The suffix -ed can be pronounced in three different ways depending on the word. This can be difficult when children come to spelling these words. Let's make it easier by learning the rules!

What you need

White board and dry erase marker

Mirror

Preparation

No preparation is needed for this activity.

Activity

Look at each of the words in the list below and explore how they sound when spoken aloud. Provide your child with a mirror and allow them to say the words into the mirror so they can watch what their mouths do with each word.

What sounds do they hear when they say each word aloud? Write the words out for your child to see. See how the spelling matches the spoken sounds. Explore this with each sound and watch as your child learns to spell the words with the new knowledge they now have!

IDEA BANK

-id (ends in a 'd' or 't')	-d (voice)	-t (unvoicd)
ended	played	kissed
wanted	loved	asked
needed	enjoyed	jumped
started	called	laughed
waited	changed	danced

TOP TIPS

The -ed ending in English has three different pronunciations because of phonological rules. These rules are based on the final sound of the verb:

-id: when the verb ends in a t or d sound. This is because adding another t/d would be difficult to articulate, so a vowel sound is inserted. For example ended, wanted.

-d: when the verb ends in a voiced consonant or a vowel sound. Voiced consonants are sounds produced with vibration of the vocal cords. For example played, loved, enjoyed.

-t: when the verb ends in an unvoiced consonant. Unvoiced consonants are sounds produced without vibration of the vocal cords. For example asked, jumped, laughed.

-id	-d	-t
ended	loved	kissed

'Fix' Words

This activity focuses on Prefixes and Suffixes. Let's look at root words and add a prefix or a suffix to change it. Does your child know the difference between a prefix and suffix? Well let's find out!

What you need

Craft sticks

Pens

Tape

Preparation

Break or cut approximately ten craft sticks into three equal segments.

Write the prefixes, root words and suffixes from the idea bank below on the broken sticks.

Activity

In this activity your child needs to 'FIX' the sticks with the tape! Can they add a prefix or suffix to the root word to fix it? You can add both a prefix and suffix to some of the words and they will still make sense. Explore the words together.

TOP TIPS

A suffix is a letter or a group of letters attached to the **end** of a root word to form a new word, the most common suffixes are: -s, -es, -ing, -ed, -able, -ly.

A prefix is a letter or a group of letters attached to the **beginning** of a word, the most common prefixes are: un-, re-, dis-.

IDEA BANK

prefix	root word	suffix
re-	play	-ing
un-	happy	-iness
un-	help	-ful
un-	care	-less
re-	read	-er
over-	look	-ed
be-	friend	-ship

play ful

Suffix Puzzles

This activity focuses on Suffixes. Your child will build some words using root words and suffixes. Some may not make sense so make sure you read the words carefully.

Preparation

Write all six of the suffixes onto building blocks.

Write the root words onto separate building blocks.

What you need

Duplo, Mega Bloks or other building blocks

Dry erase marker

Activity

Encourage your child to explore bringing the root words together with a suffix to change the meaning. Play around with adding different suffixes and explore what they mean and what tense they are. For example: jump can become jumps, jumping or jumped.

TOP TIPS

Here are some rules to help you to choose the correct suffix:

-s: simply add -s to the base word if it ends in a vowel or a voiced consonant (b, d, g, k, l, m, n, r, v). For example, cats, dogs, books.

-es: add -es to the base word if it ends in s, x, z, ch, sh or a consonant + y.

-ing: for CVC words, double the final consonant before adding -ing. For example, running, hopping.

-able: just add -able to the base word without changes.

-ly: simply add -ly to adjectives to form adverbs.

IDEA BANK

-s	-es	-ing
cats	boxes	running
dogs	brushes	jumping
birds	watches	eating
books	classes	sleeping
boys	dresses	reading

-ed	-able	-ly
played	comfortable	quickly
jumped	adjustable	happily
walked	reliable	slowly
looked	understandable	loudly
talked	enjoyable	nicely

comfort able

quick ly

Post-it Pull

This activity focuses on Suffixes and Prefixes. When looking at suffixes and prefixes, it's important to make note of the spelling rules and tricks we can learn along the way. When adding a prefix, the root word never changes, but when adding a suffix there are lots of changes that occur. Remind yourself of the rules on page 244 and correct each of the Post-it notes as you see them.

What you need

Post-it notes

Pens

Preparation

Write each of the root words on Post-it notes in the order presented opposite. Place them on top of one another in a pile.

To the left of the pile make a new pile with all the prefixes opposite. You need three -un Post-its, three -dis Post-its and three -re Post-its. Place them on top of each other in the order opposite.

To the right of the root words, make a new pile with all the suffixes. You need two -ly Post-its, three -ed Post-its and four -ing Post-its. Place them on top of one another in the order shown. The first word presented in three piles should say un-happy-ly.

Activity

Prompt your child to read the three Post-it notes in front of them. Discuss whether this word is spelled correctly. What do you do to the y when adding -ly? You take off the y and add ily. Provide your child with a pen to make the correction on the root word.

Now, remove the root word and see what word is presented. Is this spelled correctly? Continue to explore as you pull away the Post-it notes.

TOP TIPS

When looking at the root words, make sure you and your child look at the spelling error that occurs when you add the suffix.

Grab a pen and cross out the letter you do not need or add a letter that you do need.

This will support the spelling accuracy of suffixes going forwards!

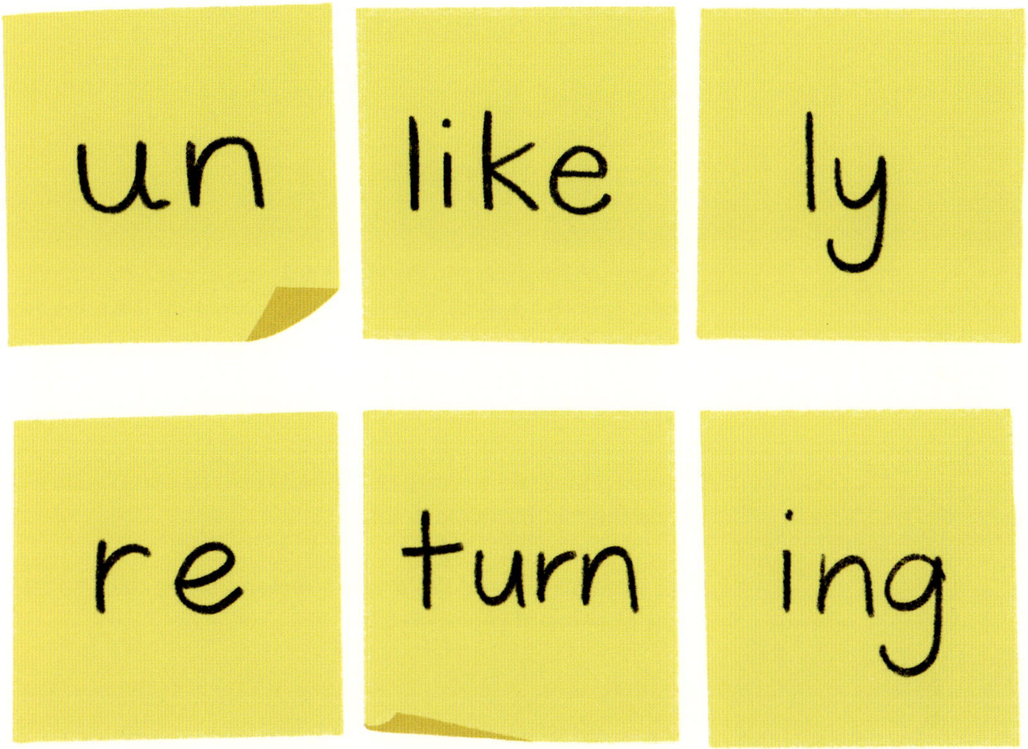

un like ly

re turn ing

IDEA BANK

prefix	root word	suffix
un	happy	ly
un	like	ly
un	pack	ed
dis	agreed	ed
dis	approve	ed
dis	connect	ing
re	turn	ing
re	write	ing
re	play	ing

Rule Book

This activity focuses on Spelling Rules. Have you heard of the Spelling Police? No? Well, they have a very special rule book that they use all the time. In this rule book, each of the spelling rules are presented very clearly! Your child can make their own Rule Book and become a member of the Spelling Police!

What you need

Pencil

Paper

Preparation

No preparation is needed for this activity.

Activity

Tell your child all about the Rule Book and explain that it will be a useful tool to have, so that they never forget all the rules. Before prompting them or reminding them of any of the rules you have learned so far, see what they know and what they remember. There are so many rules to choose from.

Prompt your child to write as many of the rules as possible and place them into their Rule Book.

There are also lots of fun ways to remember the rules so try to think of some of your own too!

TOP TIPS

Add -ed for past tense and -ing for present continuous tense.

Double the final consonant before adding -ed or -ing if the verb follows a CVC pattern. For example, hop, hopped, hopping.

If the word ends in a consonant followed by -y, change -y to -i before adding -ed or -ly. For example, carry/carried, lucky/luckily.

When to use a c or k? Use c for words that begin with a, o and u. For example, cat, coat, cut. Use k for the e and i. For example, kite, kept, kit.

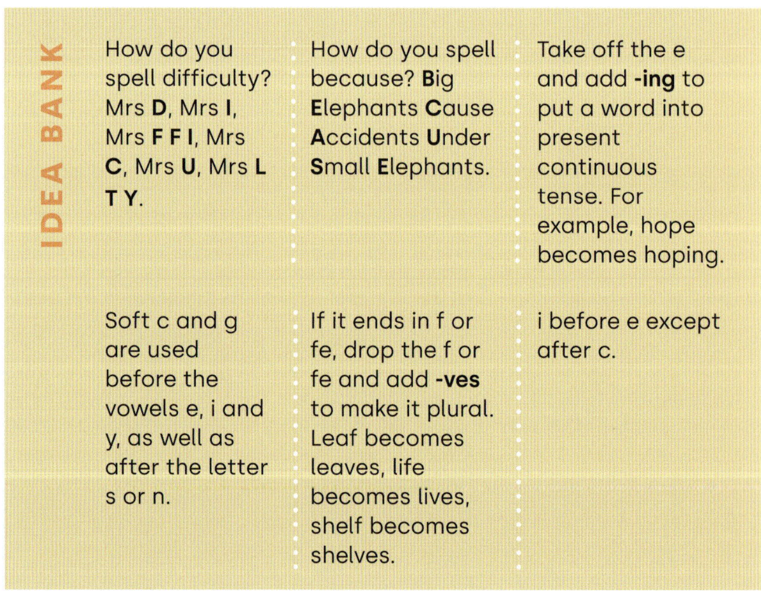

IDEA BANK

How do you spell difficulty? Mrs **D**, Mrs **I**, Mrs **F F I**, Mrs **C**, Mrs **U**, Mrs **L T Y**.

How do you spell because? **B**ig **E**lephants **C**ause **A**ccidents **U**nder **S**mall **E**lephants.

Take off the e and add **-ing** to put a word into present continuous tense. For example, hope becomes hoping.

Soft c and g are used before the vowels e, i and y, as well as after the letter s or n.

If it ends in f or fe, drop the f or fe and add **-ves** to make it plural. Leaf becomes leaves, life becomes lives, shelf becomes shelves.

i before e except after c.

RULE
book

Fancy Word of the Day

This activity focuses on Vocabulary and Spelling Accuracy. Use a dictionary and thesaurus to learn a fancy word of the day. Find a word you have not heard of or do not know the meaning of and find out about it.

TOP TIPS

Learning new and exciting vocabulary can offer lots of benefits for children:

A richer vocabulary allows children to express themselves more clearly and effectively.

Exposure to new words helps children understand texts more comprehensively.

When children have a diverse vocabulary, their writing becomes more engaging and expressive.

Learning new vocabulary stimulates cognitive development.

Mastering new words gives children a sense of accomplishment and boosts their confidence.

Children who can understand and use a wide range of words tend to be more confident when approaching different languages, arts and science.

Learning new vocabulary exposes children to different cultures and languages as they learn about where words originated from.

Building a solid vocabulary foundation in early childhood sets the stage for continued language development and lifelong learning.

What you need

Dictionary

White board

Dry erase marker

Preparation

Designate a time to do this daily. Try to fit it into your daily routine. We choose to do this during breakfast time and the children love it!

Activity

Simply flick through the dictionary and find a new and exciting word.

Write the word on the white board and explore what you know about the word.

Look at where it originated from, how it is spelled, how you can use it in a sentence and of course what it means.

Quite often we find some weird and wonderful words that we will use for the rest of the day.

IDEA BANK

Here are some of our favourite words: discombobulated, bioluminescent, galactic, melancholy.

Word of the day:
He was too
to speak as he won
prize.

Plural Drop

This activity focuses on Plurals. Plurals can be made in three different ways by adding -es, -s or -ies. Practise reading the words and dropping them into the correct cup!

What you need

- Three cups
- Three cardboard tubes
- Paper
- Pens
- Tape

Preparation

Write the three different plurals on the outside of the cups.

Attach each cardboard tube to a cup with tape, so that anything you post drops into the cup. Or you could put the cup by a wall and attach the tube to the wall.

Write each of the words from the idea bank below on a slip of paper.

Activity

Ask your child to read the words on the slips of paper, roll them into a ball and drop them into the correct spelling cup. Make sure they look closely at the word endings. If you would like to add an extra challenge for your child, write the words without their plural endings e.g. box instead of boxes and get them to sort them into the correct Plural Drop.

IDEA BANK

-es	-s	-ies
boxes	cats	babies
foxes	dogs	parties
matches	books	countries
wishes	chairs	families
brushes	cars	stories
churches	stars	cookies
tomatoes	rivers	pennies
heroes	computers	cherries
potatoes	teachers	ponies

TOP TIPS

-s plural rule
Most nouns form their plural by simply adding -s to the end. For example, cats, dogs, books.

-es plural rule
Nouns ending in sibilant sounds (**s**, **x**, **z**, **sh**, **ch**) or sounds that require an additional syllable use -es. For example, buses, boxes, wishes, churches.

-ies plural rule
Nouns ending in a consonant followed by y change the -y to -ies. For example, babies, parties, countries.

-e plural rule
Nouns ending in a silent -e typically just add -s. For example, cakes, makes.

-ies
-es
potato

Irregular Plurals

This activity focuses on Plurals. Some words do not follow the rules and the plurals can be tricky. Explore these irregular plurals by matching the root word with its irregular plural form.

What you need

Post-it notes

Pens

Preparation

Write the words on the Post-it notes.

Activity

Spread the Post-it notes on a flat surface, face down.

Explain that a plural is when a singular becomes a group. Some plurals can be a little trickier to understand because they sound different from the root word. Explore the words by turning them over two at a time. Try to find a matching pair. The words are a matching pair when you find the root word and the irregular plural form e.g. child and children.

TOP TIPS

Regular plurals in English typically follow predictable patterns, while irregular plurals do not follow these patterns and must be learned individually.

Irregular plurals often reflect older forms of English or have unique historical reasons for their irregularity. So, when introducing these words to your children, explain that they are old words. Try making it fun by using different voices.

IDEA BANK

root word	irregular plural
child	children
man	men
woman	women
person	people
foot	feet
tooth	teeth
mouse	mice
ox	oxen

tooth
teeth
men
foot

Speed Read

This activity focuses on Fluency. How many pompoms can you collect? Speed reading can be tricky but it's a fun skill to learn. Win a pompom for every word you read!

What you need

Flashcards or a book

Pompoms

Jar

Preparation

You can complete this activity with a book or with sight word flashcards. You could make your own flashcards with more complex words or look at a magazine or comic.

Activity

Place a pompom in the jar for every word your child reads. It really is as simple as that.

If you want to work on building speed, enjoy the same book or flashcards multiple times and see how quickly you can fill up the jar!

This activity aims to work on fluency, but it can get children in a bit of a fluster. Here are some tips to make sure they are speedy reading in the best possible way:

- Make sure they breathe between words.
- Tell them to look at each word and spot the tricky sounds first.
- Tell them to sound out or decode in their head and then read the word aloud.
- Encourage them to have fun.

TOP TIPS

Speed reading in Phase 6 phonics helps children transition from learning to read to reading to learn. It promotes fluency, automatic word recognition, comprehension skills, confidence and overall reading proficiency, setting them up for success in their ongoing literacy development.

Tally Chart Read

This activity focuses on Fluency. Search and find games can be fun – think of this like a giant word hunt. Write a list of words and see how many times your child can spot them in your book!

What you need

Book

White board

Dry erase marker

Preparation

Draw a table like the one opposite on a white board with some selected words. Ideally choose some of the high-frequency words from the idea bank below; this will get your child working hard.

Activity

While reading your child's favourite story book or a schoolbook, prompt your child to keep a tally of how many times your selected words come up. Which word will be used the most in the book?

Which word is used the least? This slows their reading down and makes them focus on sentence structure and the use of vocabulary.

IDEA BANK

Fifty high-frequency words

a, about, all, an, and, are, as, at, be, been, but, by, can, come, could, day, did, do, down, each, find, first, for, from, get, go, had, has, have, he, her, him, his, how, I, if, in, is, it, just, like, long, look, made, make, many, me, more, my, no

Word	Tally
there	~~IIII~~ I
their	I
they're	III
to	~~IIII~~ IIII
and	~~IIII~~ ~~IIII~~ I
he	IIII

Backwards Reading

This activity focuses on Spelling Patterns and Fluency. Practise proofreading your work. Proofreading is about checking for spelling errors.

What you need

White board

Dry erase marker

Tiny pompoms

Preparation

Write out one of the short paragraphs below on a white board.

Activity

Prompt your child to read the paragraph. Their job is to become the spelling and grammar police. Encourage them to put a tiny pompom on each of the spelling mistakes they spot. Can they go back and change them to the correct spelling?

TOP TIPS

This activity is best completed with your child's own work. It is good to get into the habit of proofreading your work and checking for spelling and punctuation errors.

By reading the sentence backwards, one word at a time, you can isolate each word and no longer see it within a sentence, therefore spotting spelling errors more readily.

Make sure your child is not reading each word backwards; the aim is to read the sentence one word at a time.

IDEA BANK

Paragraph 1

Once upon a tyme, in a mystikal forest, there lived a famlie of friendlee gnomes. Thair home was nestld at the foot of a tall, anciant oak tree. The gnomes luvd to explor the forest, findin new and xciting places to play hide-and-seek.

Paragraph 2

One sunny dae, the yungest gnome, Lila, decidid to ventur deeper into the forest than evr befor. She packt a smol bag with snackes and her favorit book, then set of on her adventur. Along the wa, she spottd a grup of colorfull butterflies fluttering around a patch of wildflowers.

Paragraph 3

As she walkd furthr, Lila herd a faint rustling noize behind a large bolder. Curiositie getting the best of her, she carefully approachd and peekd around the edge. To her surpriez, she saw a baby fox stuck in a thorn bush, whimpering softly.

The dog ate all the food on the table.

← Start here!

Word Trees

This activity focuses on Prefixes and Suffixes. The branches have some wonderful root words on them, but let's add some beautiful leaves as well. Get your child to use what they know about prefixes and suffixes and add them on the leaves.

What you need

A large piece of paper

Paint sticks or coloured pens

Green paper

Scissors

Preparation

Draw a tree on a piece of paper. Write the root words from the idea bank below on the branches.

Cut some leaves out of the green paper.

Activity

Provide your child with the green leaves and a pen. Can your child add some prefixes or suffixes to the tree to change the words on the branches?

This visual aid shows that the leaves are changing each of the branches just by adding a few words!

IDEA BANK

prefixes	root words	suffixes
de- (opposite of)	act	-able /-ible (able to be)
en- (put into)	create	-al (relating to)
inter- (between)	manage	-er /-or (one who)
mis- (wrongly)	appear	-ful (full of)
non- (not)	happy	-ing (action or process)
pre- (before)	decide	-ish (like, somewhat)
re- (again)	play	-less (without)
sub- (under)	connect	-ly (in a manner of)
un- (not)	agree	-ment (action or result)
	comfort	-tion /-sion (act or state of)

re
turn
ly
friend
un
kind
non
sense
ful
cheer
ing
manage
ed
play
happy
un
ing
act
slow
ly

Tricky Bit Spotter

This activity focuses on Fluency and Accuracy. Decoding long and complicated words can be tricky, but finding the tricky part of the word is the easiest bit! Let's take a look at some teeny tiny words and see if a magnifying glass can help us find the tricky part.

What you need

- Magnifying glass
- Paper
- Pencil

Preparation

Write the words from the idea bank below on slips of paper as tiny as you possibly can. Lay them out on the table with the magnifying glass. (Alternatively you can print the words because writing very small can be difficult.)

Activity

Encourage your child to take a look at each of the words one by one, and use the magnifying glass to make the letters bigger. What do they notice about each of the words? They have more than one syllable. They have complex sounds and they are difficult to decode. Ask them to try spotting the tricky part of the word first and then sound out the rest. Breaking the word down helps with decoding.

TOP TIPS

When presenting these teeny tiny words for children to read, it's often good to print them using font size three.

Grab your magnifying glass and see if they can read the word.

It makes it really fun for them, like they are reading a secret sentence!

Use a magnifying glass to see if you can read the sentence above!

IDEA BANK

polysyllabic words	prefixes and suffixes
important	unhappy
celebrate	disagree
treasure	overcooked
magical	understood
sunshine	prehistoric

silent letters	adjacent consonants
comb	splash
thumb	strain
whistle	grasp
wrist	strength
castle	script

Word Chunking

This activity focuses on Reading Fluency. Chunking words is a great way to decrease cognitive load. Let's cut up some words and piece them back together to help us read!

What you need

Paper

Scissors

Pen

Preparation

Write the words from the idea bank below onto slips of paper in large writing.

Activity

Prompt your child to cut the longer words into chunks and then piece them back together. For example 'ad-ver-tise-ment'. Look at what you know about each of the chunks and discuss what rules or patterns you notice.

For an extra challenge, cut all of the words up and mix them up. Can your child create any other words with the chunks?

Important information

Here are several reasons why word chunking is beneficial for Phase 6 phonics:

- Word chunking allows children to break longer words into smaller, manageable parts or chunks.
- By recognising common chunks within words, children can read more fluently.
- As children learn common word chunks, they become more familiar with parts of words that recur frequently in the English language.
- When children can identify common chunks in words, they can spell more accurately.
- Understanding word chunks helps children comprehend the meaning of texts better.

IDEA BANK

multi-syllable words
alphabetical, opportunity, revolutionary, university, collaboration, explanation, imagination, investigation, accommodation, communication

alph
a
be
ortunity
ex
iversity
gination

Summary

'Children learn as they play. Most importantly, in play, children learn how to learn.'

O. Fred Donaldson

This quote beautifully encapsulates the idea that play is not just about having fun; it's a vital process through which children develop critical learning skills. When children engage in play, they explore, experiment and make sense of the world around them. This quote is a powerful reminder of the importance of fostering playful learning for children, no matter their age.

I hope that *Read, Write, Play* has shown you that learning together can be fun and challenging, and that learning opportunities are everywhere.

In writing this book, I wanted to ensure that phonics is as fun, engaging and challenging as it can be. Together we can make phonics playful.

Never stop playing, because through play we can learn anything!

Digraphs, Trigraphs and Actions

Sound	What is it?	Action
ch (chip)	consonant digraph	Cover your nose as if you are going to sneeze and say **ch**.
sh (shed)	consonant digraph	Put your index finger to your lips and say **sh**.
th (thin) unvoiced	consonant digraph	Place your hand to your lips and sweep down. Stretch the **th** sound and say **th**ank you.
th (the) voiced	consonant digraph	Place your hand on your neck and say **th**, feeling the vibration and the difference between the voiced **th** and the unvoiced **th**.
ng (strong)	consonant digraph	Hold your arm out and flex your muscle, saying **ng**.
ai (rain)	vowel digraph	Hold your hand up, wiggle your fingers and move your hand down to make a rain movement, saying **ai**.
ee (see)	vowel digraph	Place your hand on your forehead and look around, saying **ee**.
igh (high)	trigraph	Pretend to fly a kite high in the sky and say **igh**.
oa (goat)	vowel digraph	Place your hand on your chin and wiggle your fingers to make a goat's beard, saying **oa**.
oo (poo)	vowel digraph	Wave your hand in front of your nose and say **oo**.
oo (book)	vowel digraph	Place two hands together and pretend to open a book, saying **oo**.
ar (car)	digraph	Pretend to drive a car, saying **ar**.
or (fork)	digraph	Pretend you are holding a fork, stab your food and eat it, saying **or**.
ur (curl)	digraph	Whirl your index finger around making a curl and say **ur**.

ow (blow)	digraph	Blow air from your mouth and say **ow**.
oi (coin)	vowel digraph	Point a finger and say **oi**.
ear (hear)	trigraph	Point to your ear and say e**ar.**
air (fair)	trigraph	Wag your finger in the air and say **air**.
ure (pure)	trigraph	Pretend to mix a potion and say **ure**.
er (letter)	digraph	Pretend to post a letter in a post box, saying **er**.
ay (play)	vowel digraph	Pretend to build blocks on top of each other, saying **ay**.
ou (shout)	vowel digraph	Place both hands around your mouth and loudly say **ou**.
ow (cow)	digraph	Using both hands give yourself horns and say **ow**.
ie (tie)	vowel digraph	Pretend to fasten your tie and say **ie**.
ea (tea)	vowel digraph	Pretend to sip a cup of tea and say **ea**.
oy (toy)	digraph	Pretend to drive a toy car with your hand and say **oy**.
ir (whirl)	digraph	Wiggle your finger in the air making it whirl and twirl, saying **ir**.
ue (glue)	vowel digraph	Pretend your hands are stuck together with glue, saying **ue**.
aw (yawn)	digraph	Let out a huge yawn and say **aw**.
ew (chew)	digraph	Pretend to chew something in your mouth and say **ew**.
a-e (make)	split digraph	Pretend to hold a bowl and spoon and mix, saying **a-e**.
e-e (trapeze)	split digraph	Pretend to swing from a trapeze with both hands and say **e-e**.
i-e (smile)	split digraph	Place one finger under the mouth and make a smile shape, saying **i-e**.
o-e (phone)	split digraph	Hold your hand to your ear as if you are on the phone and say **o-e**.
u-e (huge)	split digraph	Hold your hands either side of you making yourself huge and say **u-e**.

Homemade Playdough Recipe

Playdough is simple to make and uses ingredients you will typically find in your kitchen cupboards.

Ingredients

1 cup / 120g flour

½ cup / 150g salt

2 tsp cream of tartar (optional)

1 tbsp vegetable oil

1 cup / 230ml boiling water

food colouring

Method

1 Place the flour, salt and cream of tartar in a bowl.

2 Make a well in the dry ingredients and add the vegetable oil, boiling water and food colouring if you are adding.

3 Mix well until it all comes together into a ball.

4 Knead roughly until soft and smooth. (You may need gloves as it will be very hot.)

5 Leave to cool.

Note

The cream of tartar is used to preserve the playdough. It is not essential, but your playdough may not last as long without it.

Once you have finished playing with your playdough, wrap in plastic and store in an airtight container. If stored correctly, this playdough will last you months.

·ESSENTIALS·
VEGETABLE O
·MY PANTRY·

Initial Sounds and Actions

Some sounds are stretchy and some are bouncy.

Stretchy sounds are pronounced in one continuous sound. Try stretching them for as long as you can. For example, **mmmmm**.

Bouncy sounds are said with a short, sharp gap in between each repetition, for example **d-d-d**.

In the table below, stretchy sounds are orange and bouncy sounds are green.

Sound		CVC word	Action
s	● (orange)	sun	Pinch all your fingers together and open them out like the sun saying **sssss**.
a	● (green)	ant	Wiggle your fingers on your right hand and pretend an ant is crawling, say **a**, **a**, **a**.
t	● (green)	tag	Extend both arms out and bounce the sound **t**, **t**, **t**.
p	● (green)	pen	Pinch your index finger and thumb together and pretend to draw on your other hand saying **p**, **p**, **p**.
i	● (green)	ink	Pinch your index finger and thumb together and point downwards like you are dipping ink saying **i**, **i**, **i**.
n	● (orange)	nut	Join your arms together to make an arch above your head saying **nnn**.
m	● (orange)	map	Pull your hands apart like you are looking at a map saying **mmm**.
d	● (green)	dog	Point your hands down twice to make dog paws and say **d**, **d**, **d**.
g	● (green)	gap	Pull your hands apart like you are making a gap and say **g**, **g**, **g**.
o	● (green)	ox	Hold your little finger and thumbs out on both hands and point them out from your head like horns saying **o**, **o**, **o**.
c	● (green)	cat	Pinch your thumb and index finger together on each hand, place them either side of your nose and move outwards like cat whiskers saying **c**, **c**, **c**.
k	● (green)	kick	Use both your index fingers and kick them back and forth saying **k**, **k**, **k**.

e	egg	Hold your left hand in a fist, and with two fingers on the right hand scoop out your egg, saying **e**, **e**, **e**.
u	up	Point up and say **u**, **u**, **u**.
r	rat	Grit your teeth together and shake your head as you stretch the sound **rrr**.
h	hen	Pinch your index finger and thumb together next to your mouth like a beak and say **h**, **h**, **h**.
b	bun	Hold one hand out and make an arch shape with your other hand. Place the arch on top of your flat hand making a bun and say **b**, **b**, **b**.
f	fox	Clap one hand on top of the other as you stretch the sound **ffff**.
l	lick	Hold an imaginary lollipop and stretch the sound **llll**.
j	jam	Use your index finger on your right hand to spread some jam on your left palm and say **j**, **j**, **j**.
v	van	Drive a van and make a V shape in your hand saying **vvvv**.
w	win	Fist pump like when you win and say **w**, **w**, **w**.
x	x-ray	Stand with your arms and legs apart and say **x**.
y	yum	Rub your tummy, yum! Say **y**, **y**, **y**.
z	zip	Zip up your top saying **zzz**.
qu	quiz	Roll your index fingers round and round near your head and say **qu**, **qu**, **qu**. This shows your brain is being quizzed.

Letter-Writing Prompts

Make sure you use a child-friendly font for this. Sassoon Primary font is a good font for teaching phonics.

a
Start at the top, draw a circle to the left, add a line to the right and flick.

b
Begin at the top, draw a line down, back up to the middle, then curve round to the right.

c
Begin at the top, draw a curve to the left and continue around in a circular motion.

d
Start at the top, draw a line down, back up to the middle, then curve to the left.

e
Start in the middle, draw a line to the right, then curl round to the left.

f
Start at the top, draw a line down, then take your pen off and draw a short line through the middle.

g
Begin at the top, draw a circle, then add a tail.

h
Start at the top, draw a line down, back up to the middle and then add a hump.

i
Draw a vertical line from top to bottom and put a dot at the top.

j
Begin with a line down, curl to the left and add a dot at the top.

k
Begin at the top, draw a line down, back to the middle, kick up and kick down.

l
Begin at the top, draw a straight line down.

m
Start at the top, draw a line down, then add two humps.

n
Begin at the top, draw a line down, then add a hump.

o
Start at the top, draw a circle clockwise.

p
Start at the top, draw a line down, then go back to the top and draw a circle to the right.

q
Begin at the top, draw a circle from left to right. Draw a line down and a small flick.

r
Start at the top, draw a line down, go back up to the top and draw a small curve.

s
Begin at the top, draw a curve to the left, then continue with a curve to the right.

t
Start at the top, draw a line down and curl to the right. Take your pen off, then add a horizontal line across the middle.

u
Begin at the top, draw a line down, curve to the right and back up to the top. Draw a line down and flick.

v
Begin at the top, draw a diagonal line down, then add a diagonal line up to the right.

w
Start at the top, draw a line down, then up, then down, then up.

x
Begin at the top, draw a diagonal line across to the right, then another diagonal line across to the left.

y
Begin at the top, draw a line down, curve to the right and back up to the top. Draw a line down and give it a tail.

z
Begin at the top, draw a line to the right, a diagonal line to the left and a line to the right.

Speech Sounds Description

Written by Registered Speech and Language Therapist Jenny Hillier

/a, e, i, o, u/ – For all short vowels, the tongue tip is held behind the lower teeth, while the body of the tongue is bunched. The oral cavity opens a little more for some and a little less for others. The shape of the lips also changes, depending on the vowel, for example rounded for the /o/ sound versus spread for the /e/ sound.

/p/ – Lips come together and then quickly part to release air through the mouth. Teeth are slightly open. This is a voiceless sound.

/b/ – As with the /p/ sound, lips come together and then quickly part to release air through the mouth. Teeth are slightly open. This sound is voiced (noisy).

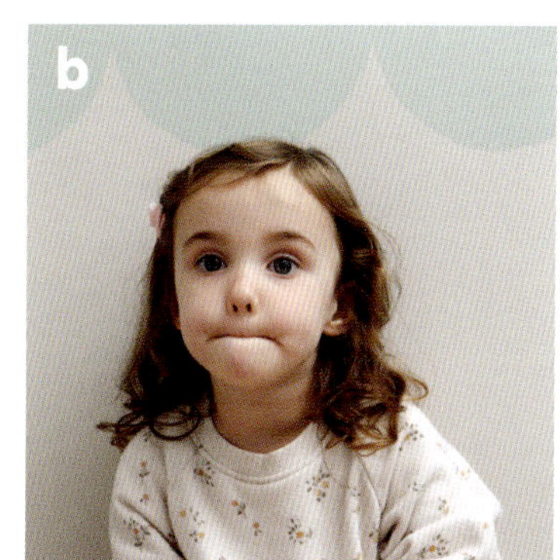

/m/ – Lips are closed and the air is released through the nose. This sound is voiced.

/n/ – The mouth is open and the tip of the tongue is touching the alveolar ridge (the small ridge just behind the top teeth). Air is released through the nose. This sound is voiced.

/t/ – The tip of the tongue touches the alveolar ridge. Air is then pushed out. This is a voiceless sound.

/d/ – As with the /t/ sound, the tip of the tongue touches the alveolar ridge. Air is then pushed out. This sound is voiced.

/ck/ – The back of the tongue raises to touch the soft palate. Mouth is open. This is a voiceless sound.

/g/ – As with the /k/ sound, the back of the tongue raises to touch the soft palate. Mouth is open. This sound is voiced.

/**h**/ – No movement of the lips or tongue is required. Mouth open and breathe out. This is a voiceless sound.

/**f**/ – Top teeth lightly touch the bottom lip. Blow air over the bottom lip. This is a voiceless sound.

/**v**/ – As with the /f/ sound, top teeth lightly touch the bottom lip. Blow air over the bottom lip. This sound is voiced.

/**sh**/ – The tongue is raised and pulled back so that the sides of the tongue touch the back teeth. Lips are rounded and front teeth come together. Air continuously flows over the centre of the tongue. This is a voiceless sound.

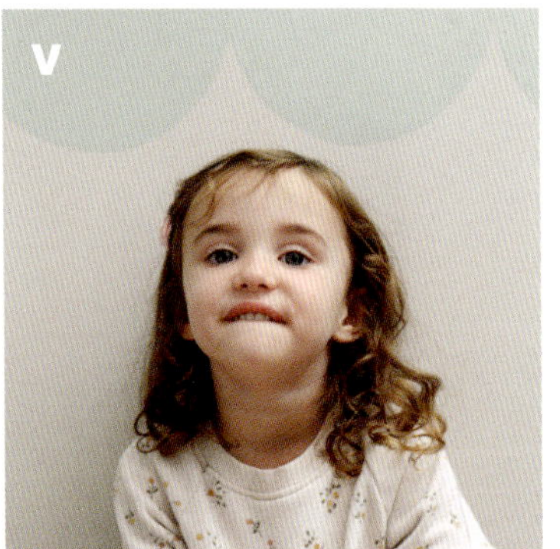

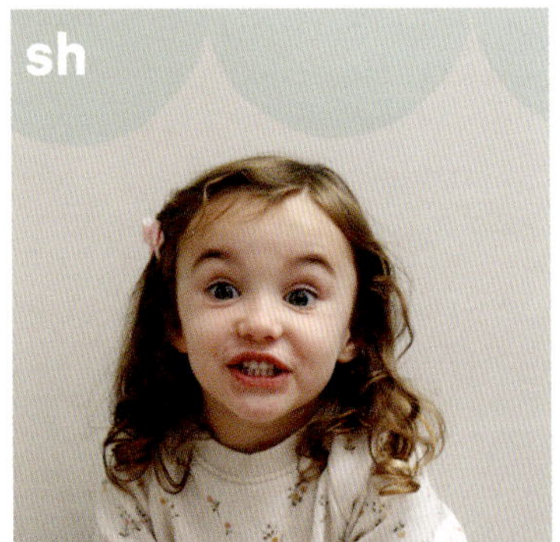

/**ch**/ – Similar position to the /sh/ sound for the tongue, lips and teeth. Air flow is more explosive for the /ch/ sound. This is also a voiceless sound.

/**j**/ – Similar position to the /sh/ and /ch/ sounds for the tongue, lips and teeth. Air flow is also quite explosive. Add your voice to differentiate between the /ch/ and /j/ sounds.

/**s**/ – The tip of the tongue lightly touches the alveolar ridge. Air continuously flows over the centre of the tongue. This is a voiceless sound.

/**z**/ – As with the /s/ sound, the tip of the tongue lightly touches the alveolar ridge. Air continuously flows over the centre of the tongue. This sound is voiced.

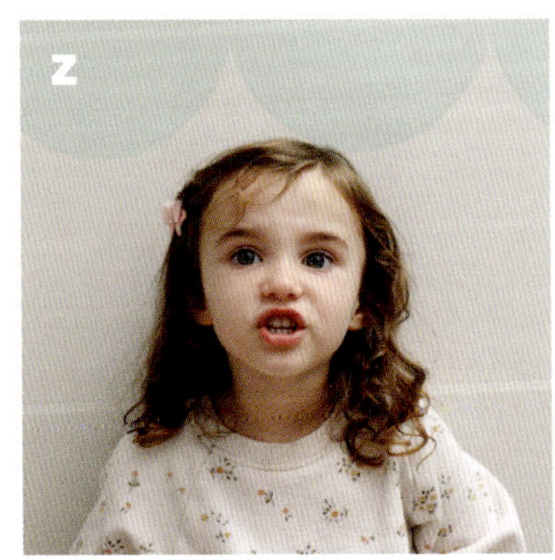

/**y**/ – The tip of the tongue sits behind the bottom front teeth. The middle of the tongue raises towards the hard palate. This sound is voiced.

/**ew**/ – Lips are rounded and the back of the tongue raises slightly towards the soft palate. This sound is voiced.

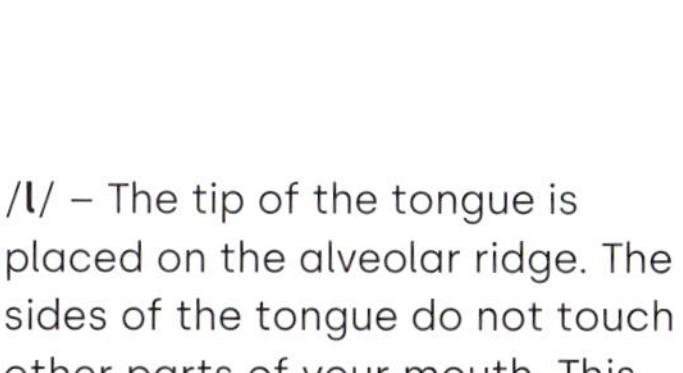

/**l**/ – The tip of the tongue is placed on the alveolar ridge. The sides of the tongue do not touch other parts of your mouth. This sound is voiced.

/**r**/ – Production varies depending on other sounds in the word. Generally, the tongue is raised up and brought back in the mouth. The tongue tip hovers in the middle of the mouth. This sound is voiced.

/**x**/ – This sound is made with the combination of a /k/ and a /s/ sound. The back of the tongue raises to touch the soft palate. The tip of the tongue then raises to lightly touch the alveolar ridge. Air flows out.

Syllable Slide

To the tune of the 'Cha-Cha Slide'.

(Clap your hands)
All right now, we're gonna do the Syllable Slide!
Let's go to work!

To the left, two syllables.
(adult says the word ti-ger/child claps twice)

Take it back, one syllable.
(adult says the word cat/child claps once)

Three syllables this time!
(adult says the word kan-ga-roo/child claps three times)

Four syllables, let's go!
(adult says the word rhi-no-cer-os/child claps four times)

Five syllables this time!
(adult says the word hi-po-po-tam-us/child claps five times)

One syllable, let's go!
(adult says the word cat/child claps once)

Two syllables, let's go!
(adult says the word ti-ger/child claps twice)

Everybody clap your hands!

Clap, clap, clap, clap your hands.
Clap, clap, clap, clap your hands.

Vowel Song

To the tune of 'Bingo Was His Name-o'.

Verse 1
There are some letters you should know,
And vowels are their name-o.
A, E, I, O, U
A, E, I, O, U
A, E, I, O, U
And vowels are their name-o.

Verse 2
The letter A is in the mix,
And vowels are their name-o.
_, E, I, O, U
_, E, I, O, U
_, E, I, O, U
And vowels are their name-o.

Verse 3
Next is E, the second vowel,
And vowels are their name-o.
_, _, I, O, U
_, _, I, O, U
_, _, I, O, U
And vowels are their name-o.

Verse 4
The letter I comes after E,
And vowels are their name-o.
_, _, _, O, U
_, _, _, O, U
_, _, _, O, U
And vowels are their name-o.

Verse 5
O comes next, it's almost last,
And vowels are their name-o.
_, _, _, _, U
_, _, _, _, U
_, _, _, _, U
And vowels are their name-o.

Verse 6
U is the last but not the least,
And vowels are their name-o.
A, E, I, O, U
A, E, I, O, U
A, E, I, O, U
And vowels are their name-o.

Acknowledgements

Firstly, nothing would be possible without my husband, Adam – his unwavering support, patience and encouragement is like no other. Thank you for being the not-so-silent partner of Little Happy Learners and believing in me, even when I didn't.

To my incredible children, Ted, Finn and Edie, thank you for being my constant inspiration and for letting me test everything out on you. Thank you for sharing your love of phonics with the world. Your enthusiasm and curiosity keep me and millions of others motivated every day.

A very special thank you has to go to the children and staff at Hayes Primary School. You taught me to love phonics and showed me the joy and impact of teaching. My years at Hayes were some of the best of my life; being a teacher was pure magic! Your dedication and passion to make learning fun will always fill me with the most wonderful memories.

To Darryl, thank you for putting up with my crazy ideas. You truly are the best.

Finally, thank you, Tom, for believing in *Read, Write, Play* and for allowing me to share my love of phonics with the world; without you and the Little, Brown team this would all just be ideas in my head.